# Pinky & Pepper Forever

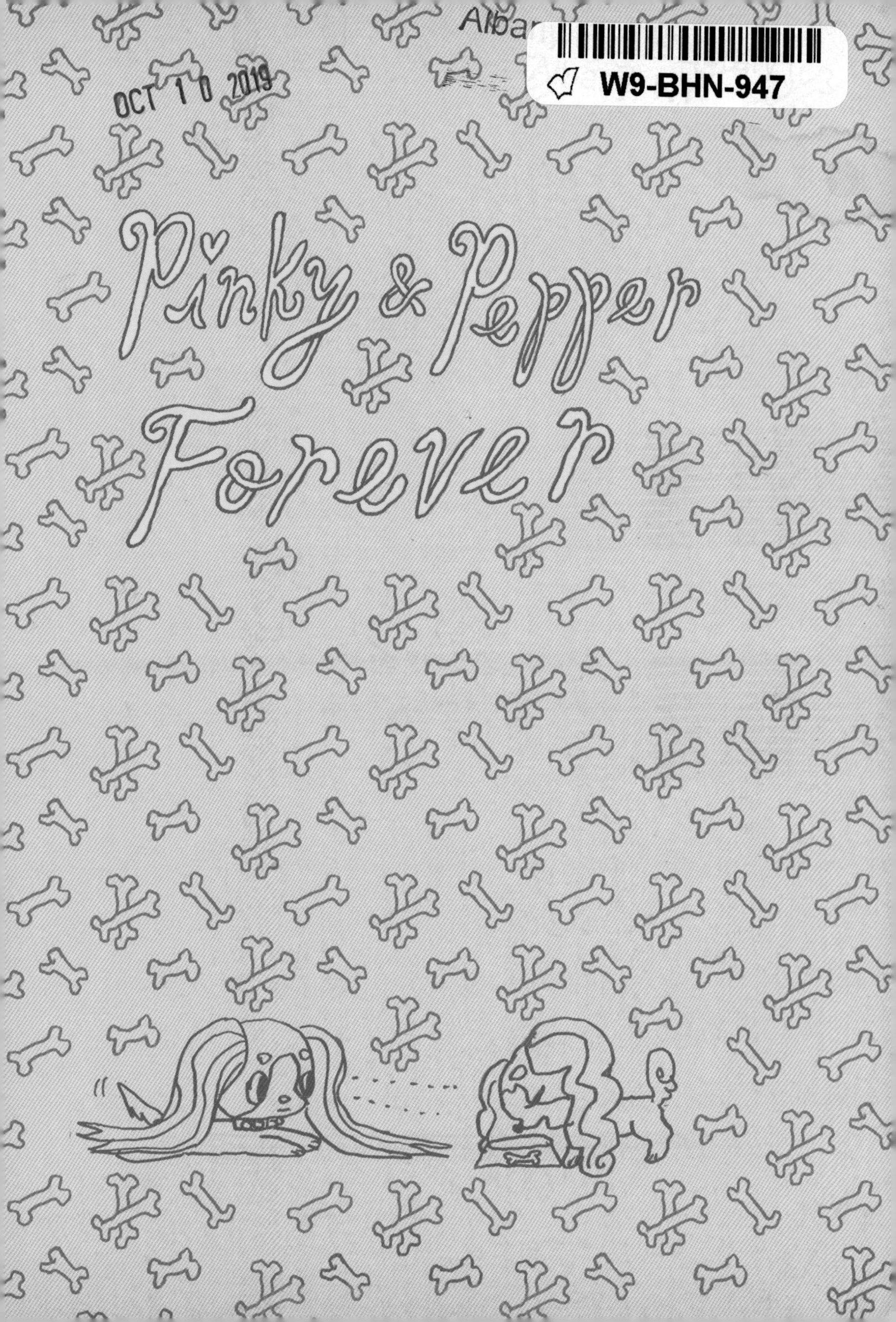

# PiNKY

**AGE:** 22
**B-DAY:** MAY 27 Ⅱ
**MAJOR:** NEW MEDIA
**LOVES:** LONG RELAXING BATHS
**PET PEEVE:** BASIC BITCHES

# PepPeR

AGE: 21
B-DAY: NOVEMBER 11 Ⓜ
MAJOR: ART HiSTORY

LOVES: DOMESTiC LiFE

PET PEEVE: SHEDDiNG

# CONTENT WARNING:

SUICIDE
TORTURE
SEXUAL THEMES
BONDAGE
CARTOON
VIOLENCE

HERE WE GO...

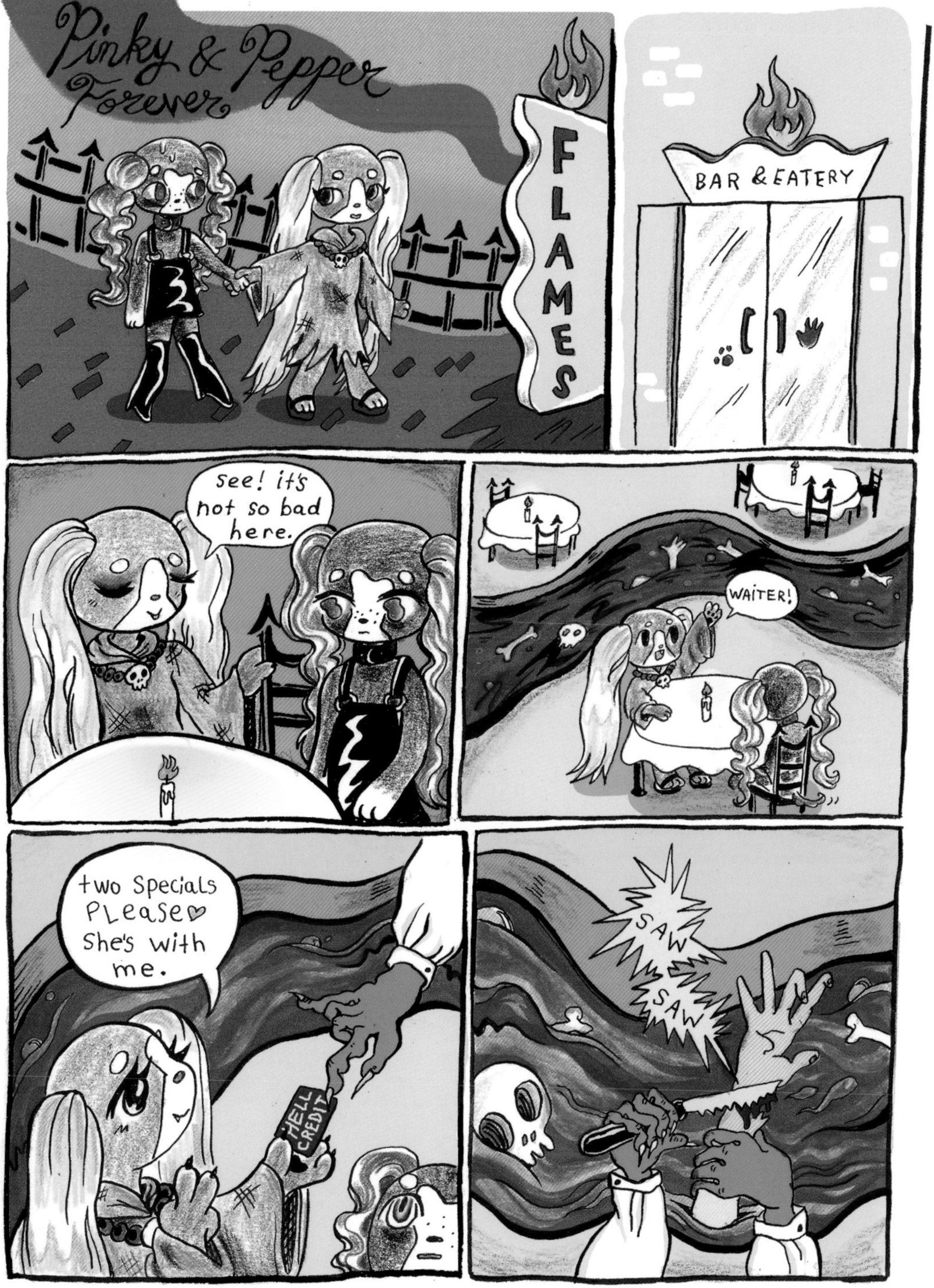
Pinky & Pepper Forever
FLAMES
BAR & EATERY
see! it's not so bad here.
WAITER!
two Specials PLease♡ She's with me.
HELL CREDIT
SAW SAW

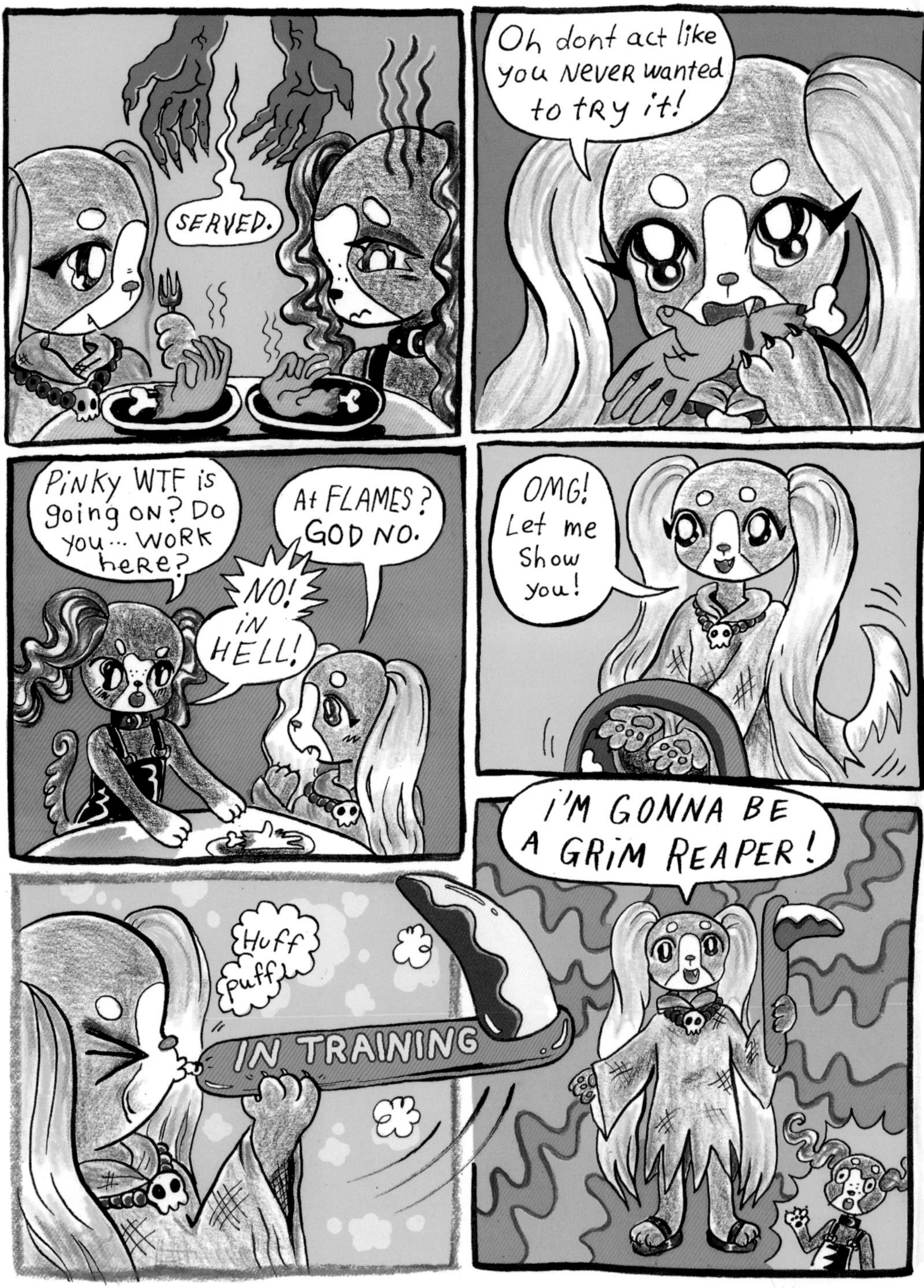
SERVED.
Oh dont act like you NEVER wanted to TRY it!
Pinky WTF is going on? Do you... WORK here?
NO! in HELL!
At FLAMES? GOD NO.
OMG! Let me Show you!
Huff puff!
IN TRAINING
I'M GONNA BE A GRIM REAPER!

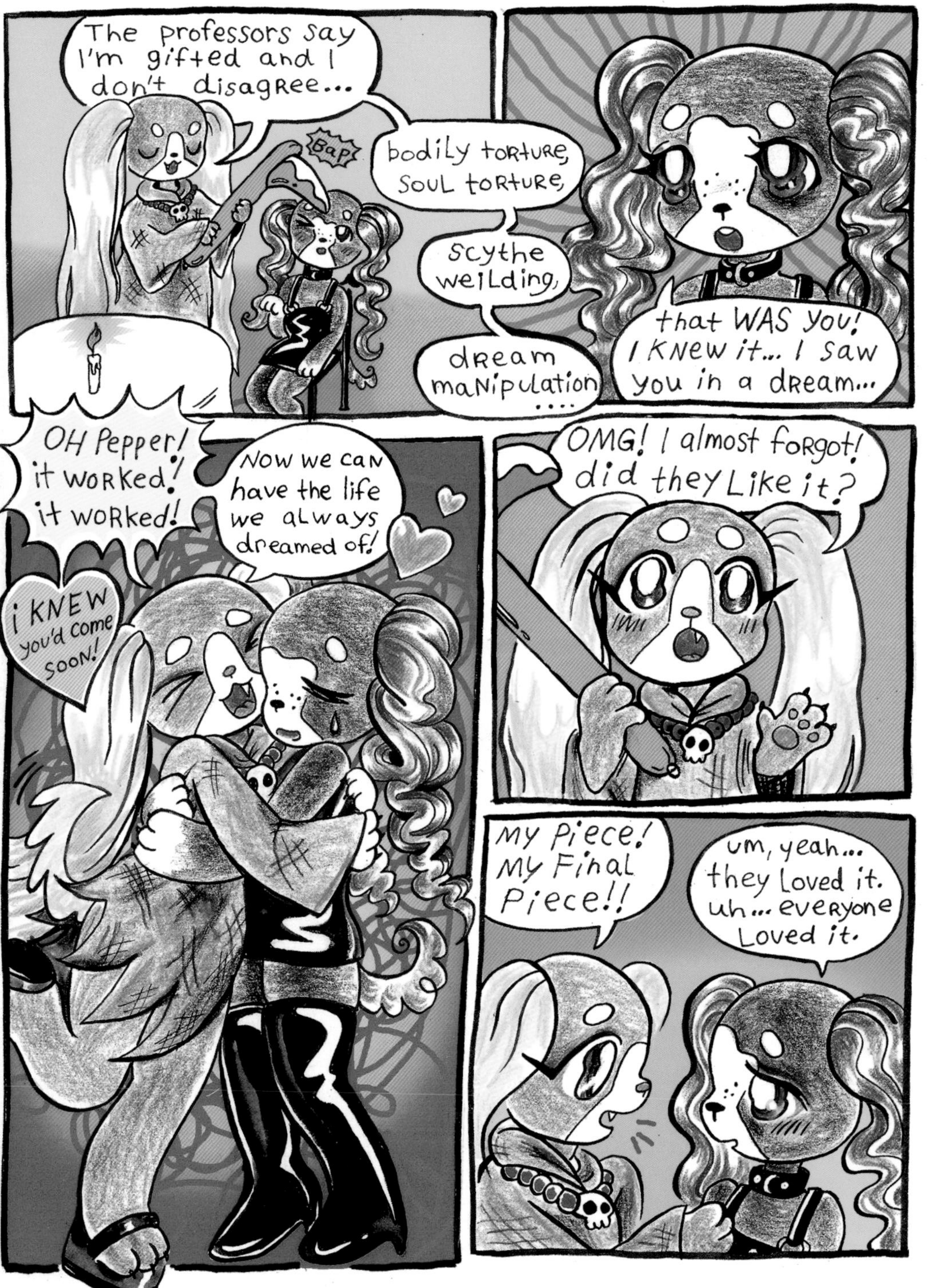

The professors say I'm gifted and I don't disagree...
Bap
bodily torture, soul torture,
scythe weilding,
dream manipulation....
that WAS you! I KNEW it... I saw you in a dream...
OH Pepper! it worked! it worked!
Now we can have the life we always dreamed of!
i KNEW you'd come soon!
OMG! I almost forgot! did they like it?
My Piece! My Final Piece!!
um, yeah... they loved it. uh... everyone loved it.

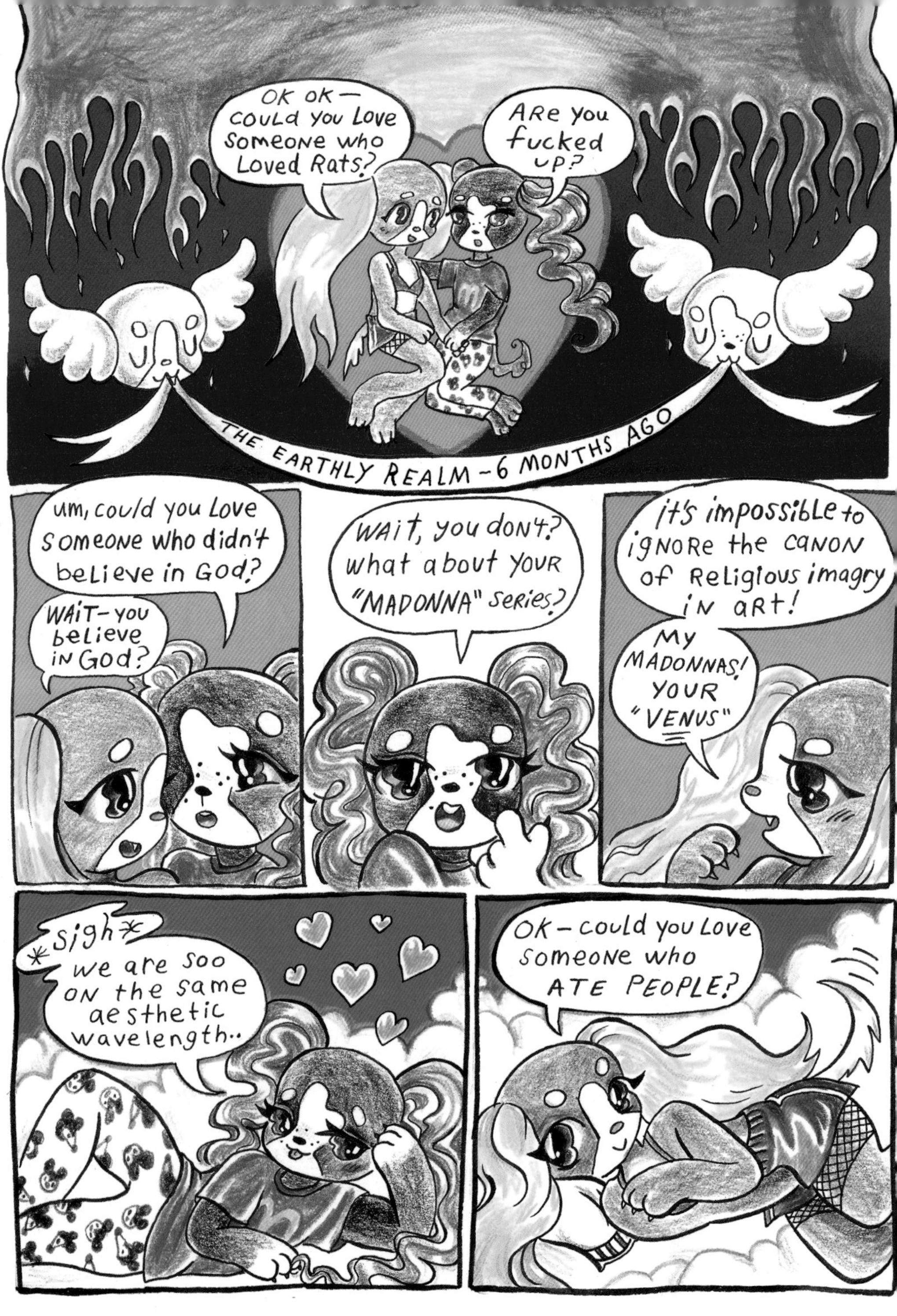

OK OK — could you Love someone who Loved Rats?
Are you fucked up?
THE EARTHLY REALM - 6 MONTHS AGO
um, could you Love someone who didn't believe in God?
WAIT — you believe in God?
WAIT, you don't? what about your "MADONNA" series?
it's impossible to ignore the canon of Religious imagry in art!
MY MADONNAS! YOUR "VENUS"
*sigh* we are soo on the same aesthetic wavelength..
OK - could you Love someone who ATE PEOPLE?

# PINKY & PEPPER FOREVER

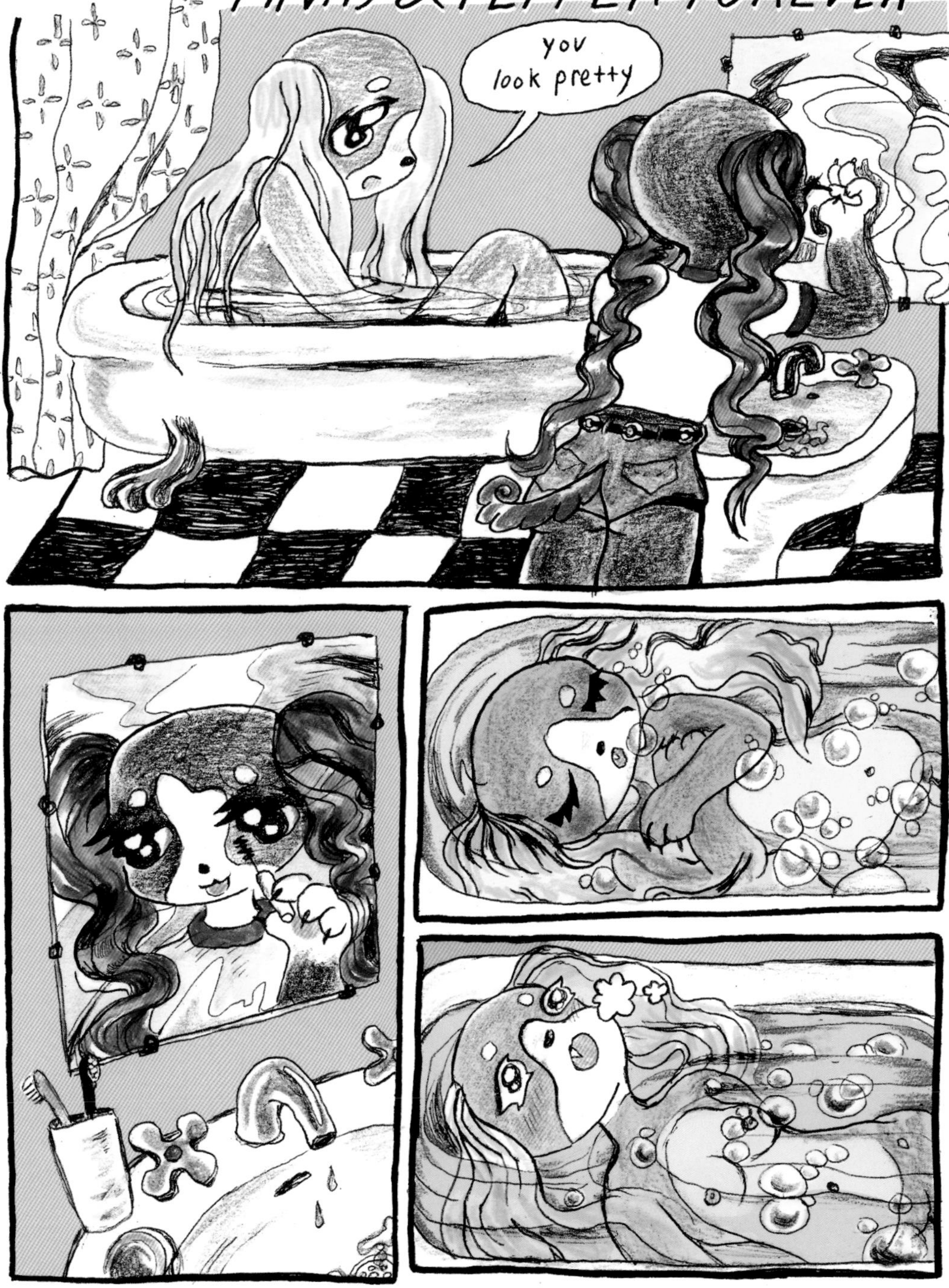
you look pretty

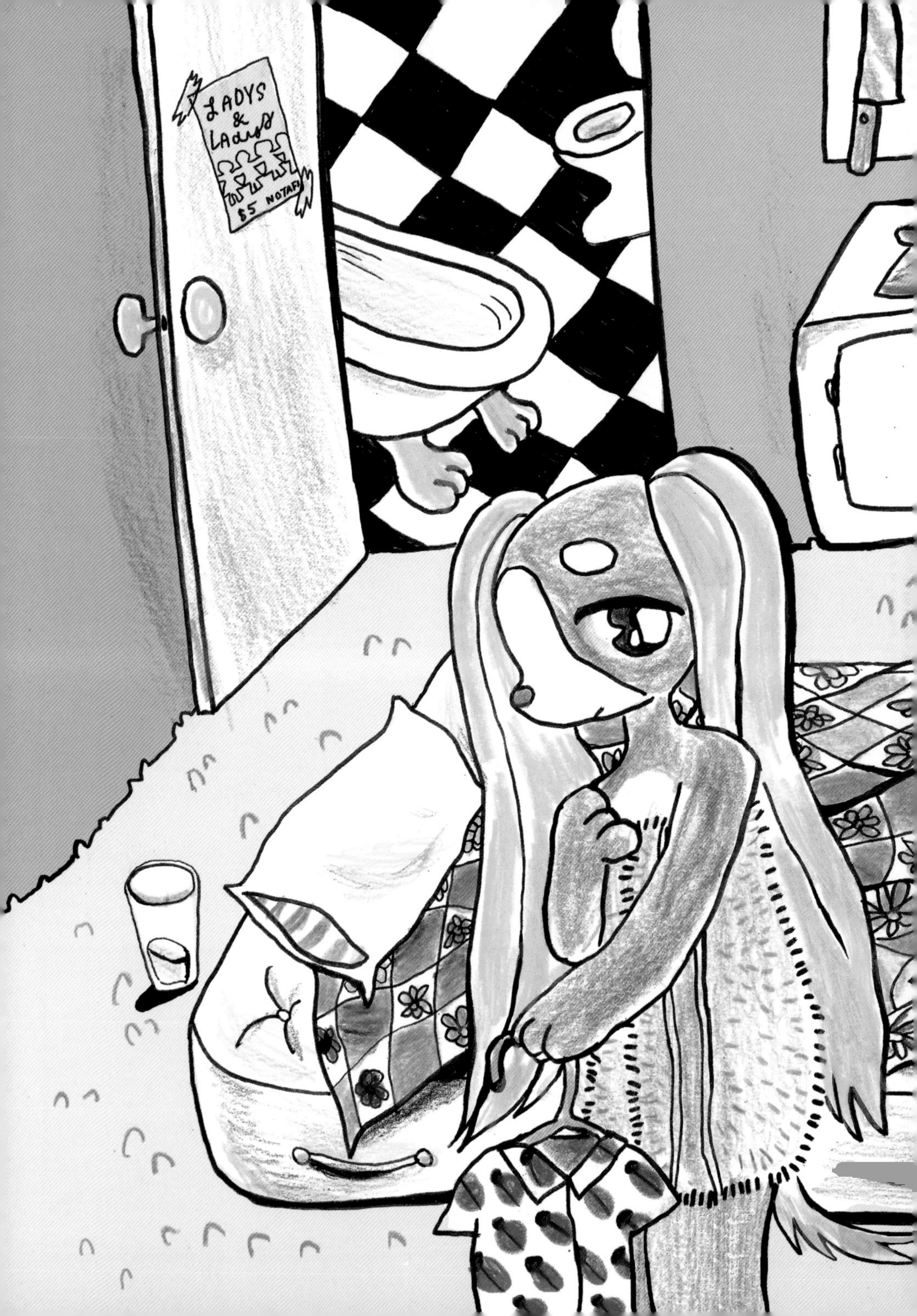
LADYS
&
Ladys
$5 NOTAFI

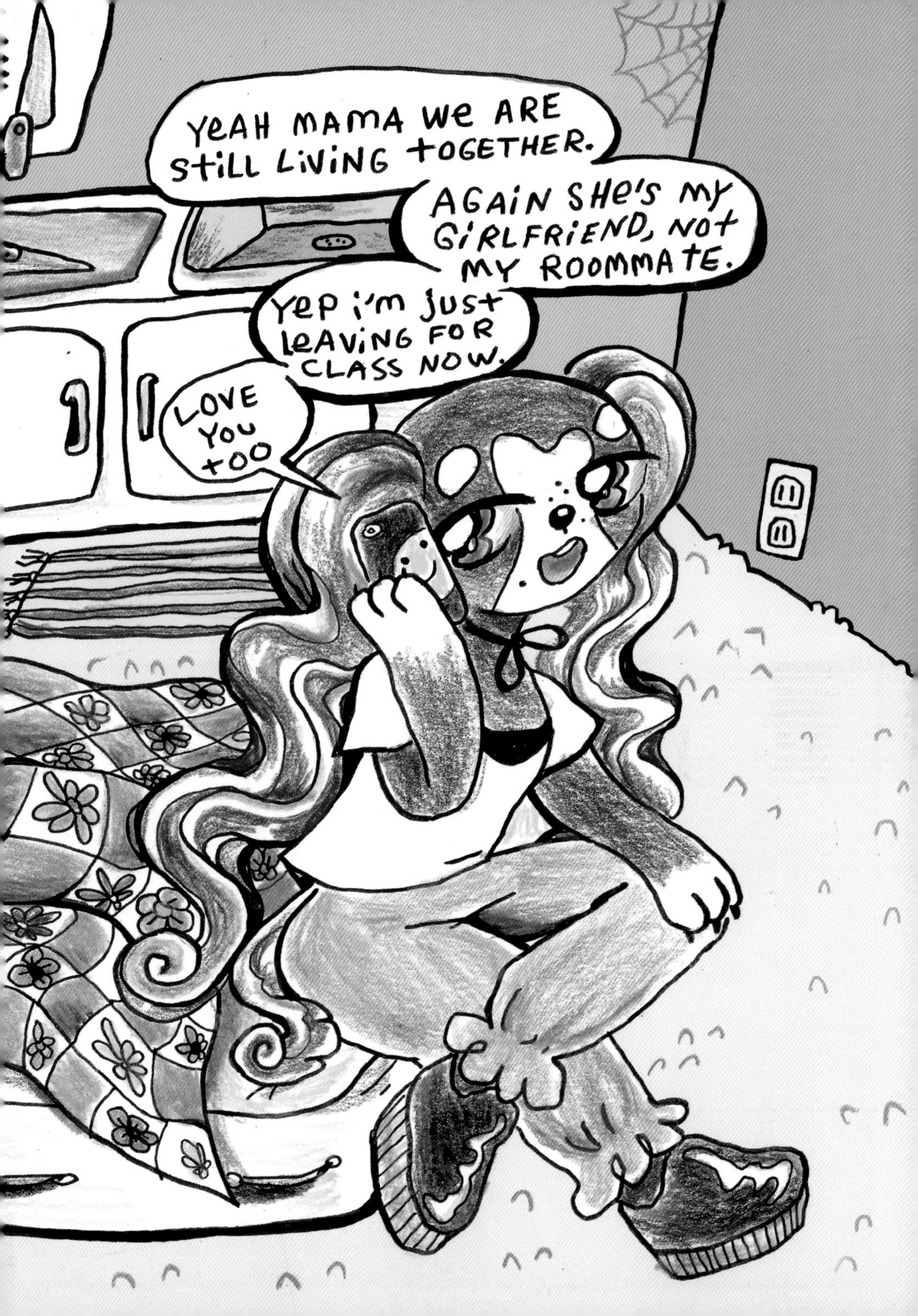
YEAH MAMA WE ARE STILL LIVING TOGETHER.
AGAIN SHE'S MY GIRLFRIEND, NOT MY ROOMMATE.
YEP I'M JUST LEAVING FOR CLASS NOW.
LOVE YOU TOO

BARKLEY COLLEGE
OF THE ARTS

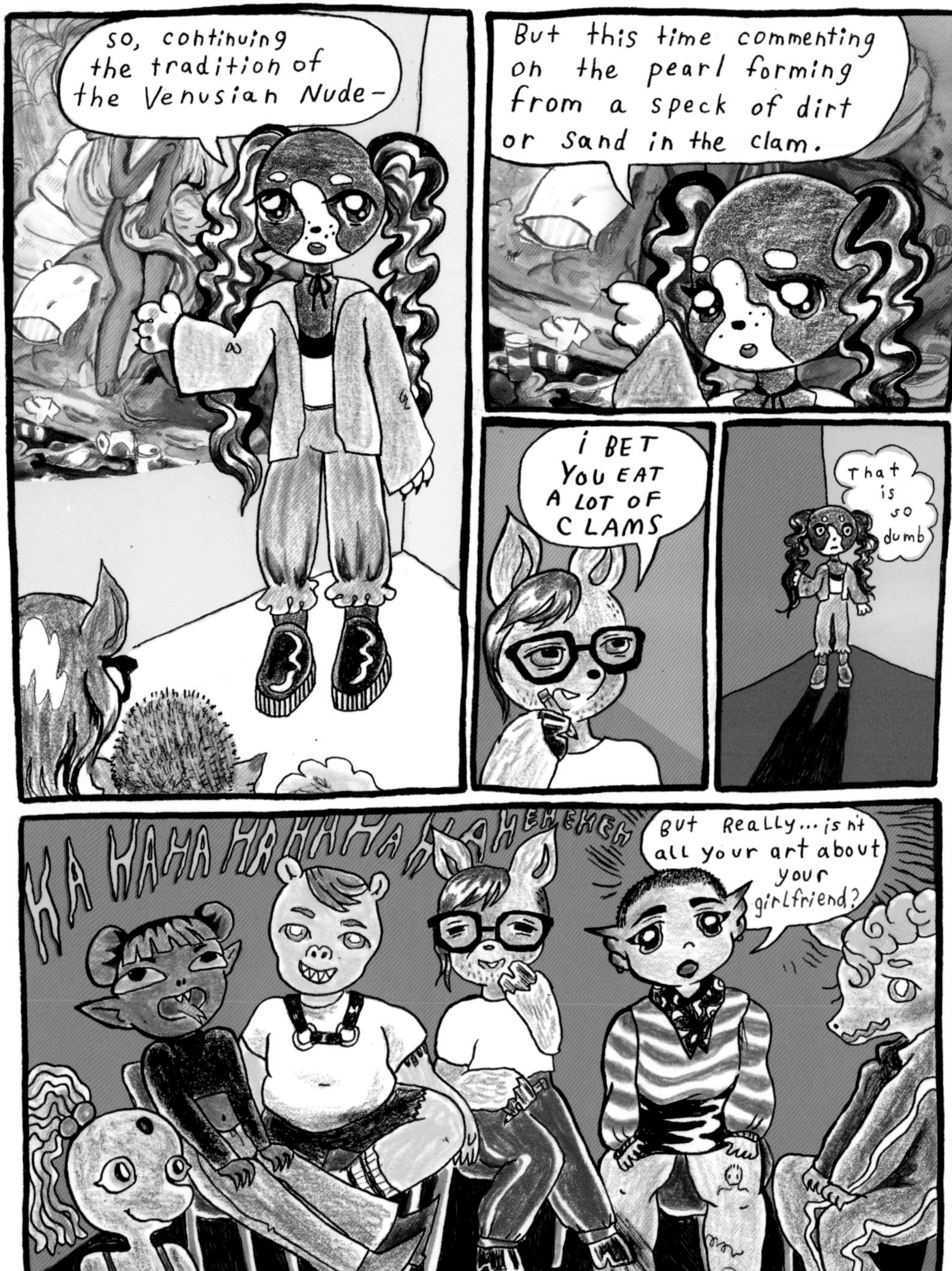
so, continuing the tradition of the Venusian Nude-
But this time commenting on the pearl forming from a speck of dirt or sand in the clam.
i BET YOU EAT A LOT OF CLAMS
That is so dumb
HA HAHA HAHAHA HAHEHEHEH
But Really... isn't all your art about your girlfriend?

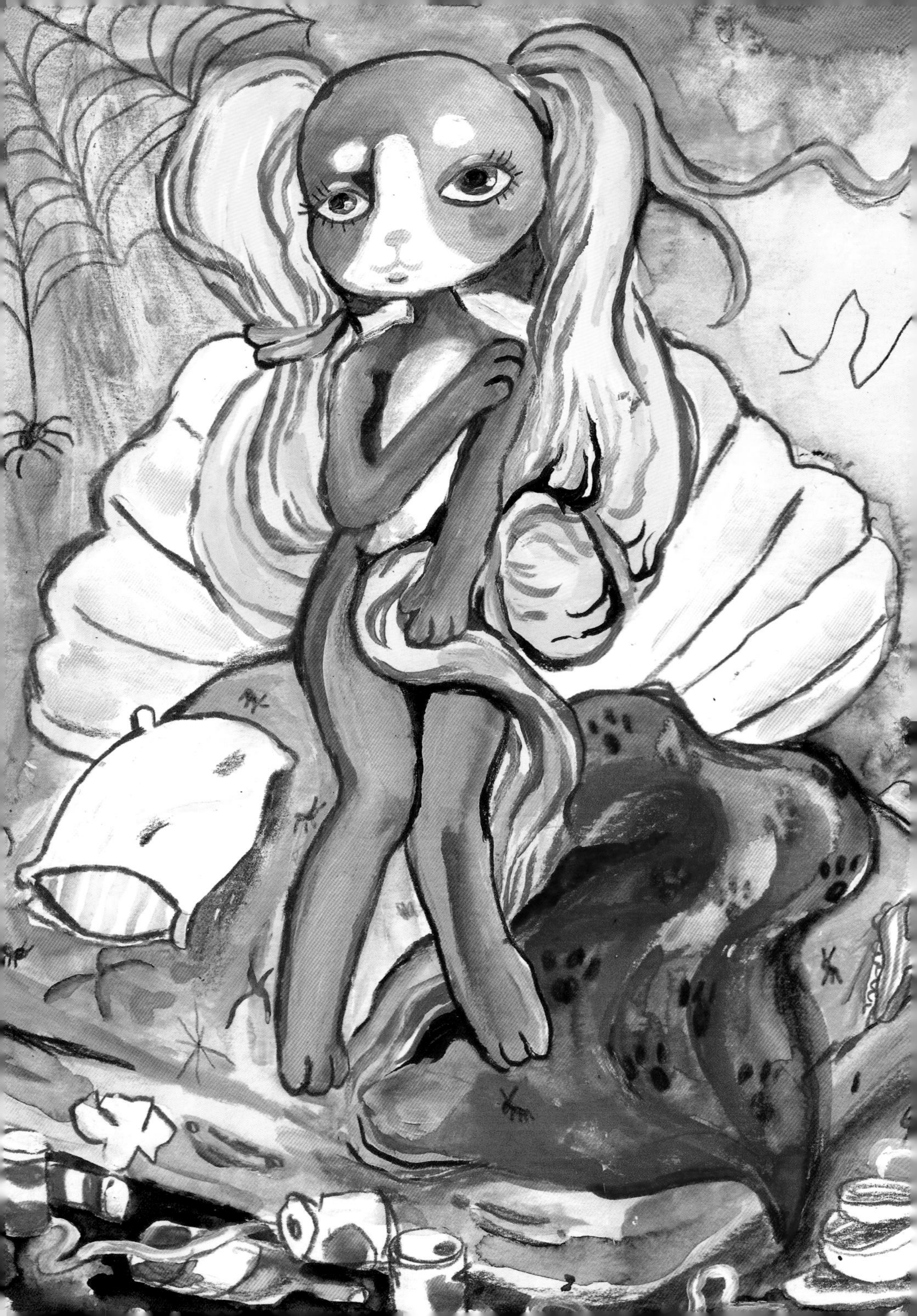

Feel like going out tonight?

SEA PARTY

Kinda 2010 but looks cute

Will any of my enemies be there?

C'mon you villian. it's a costume party! you can wear a disguise.

DIY ANGLER FISH →

MERMAID OUTFIT SHE ALREADY HAD ↓

Here, I brought a party favor

← TUNA CAN

...

Do you try to make people hate you?

Fish party, right?

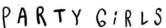

PARTY GIRLS

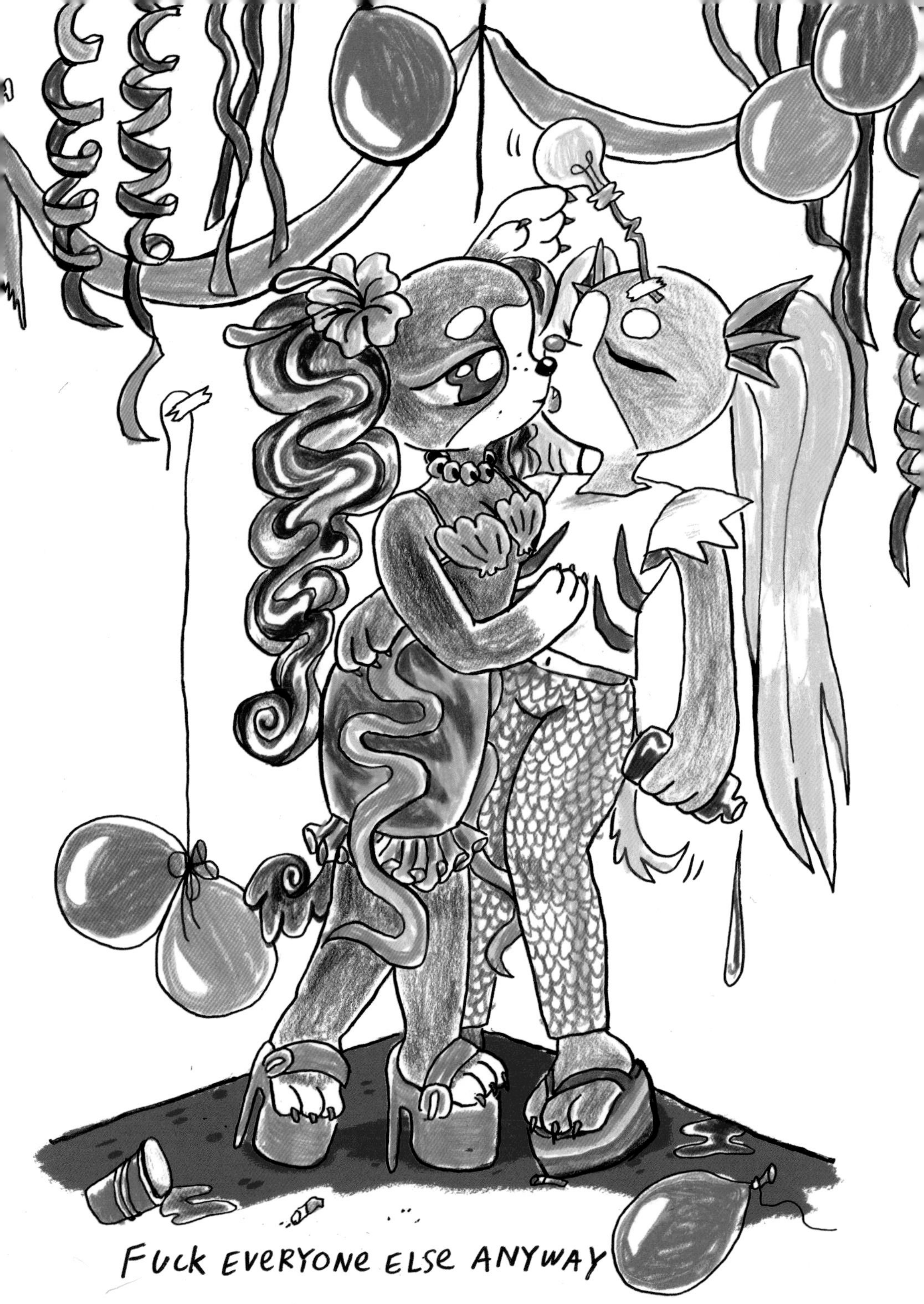
FUCK EVERYONE ELSE ANYWAY

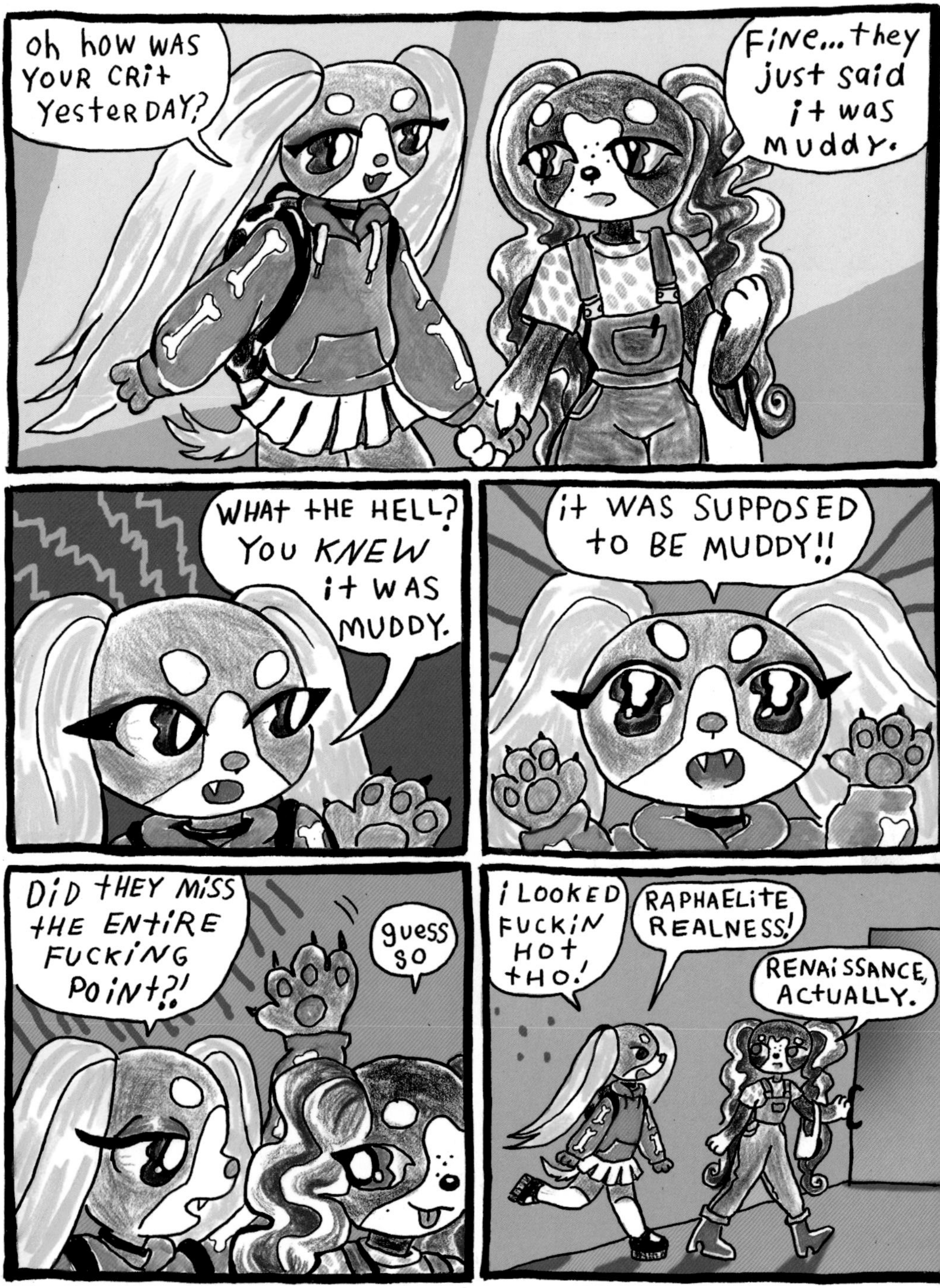
oh how WAS YOUR CRit YesterDAY?
Fine... they just said it was muddy.
WHAT tHE HELL? YOU KNEW it WAS MUDDY.
it WAS SUPPOSED to BE MUDDY!!
DiD tHEY MiSS tHE ENtiRE FUCKiNG POiNt?!
guess so
i LOOKED FUCKiN HOt, tHO!
RAPHAELitE REALNESS!
RENAiSSANCE, ACtUALLY.

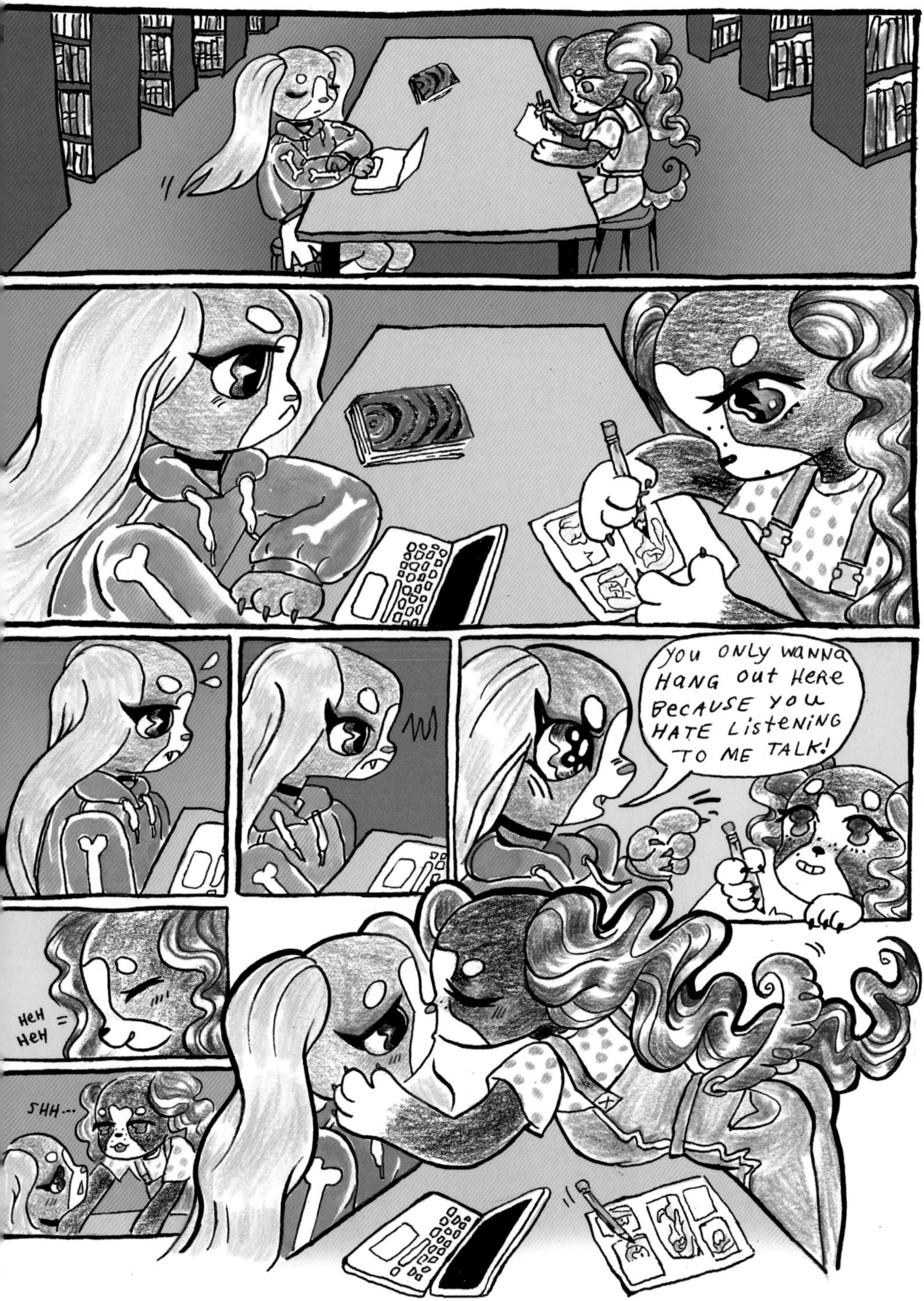

YOU ONLY WANNA HANG OUT HERE BECAUSE YOU HATE LISTENING TO ME TALK!
HEH HEH
SHH...

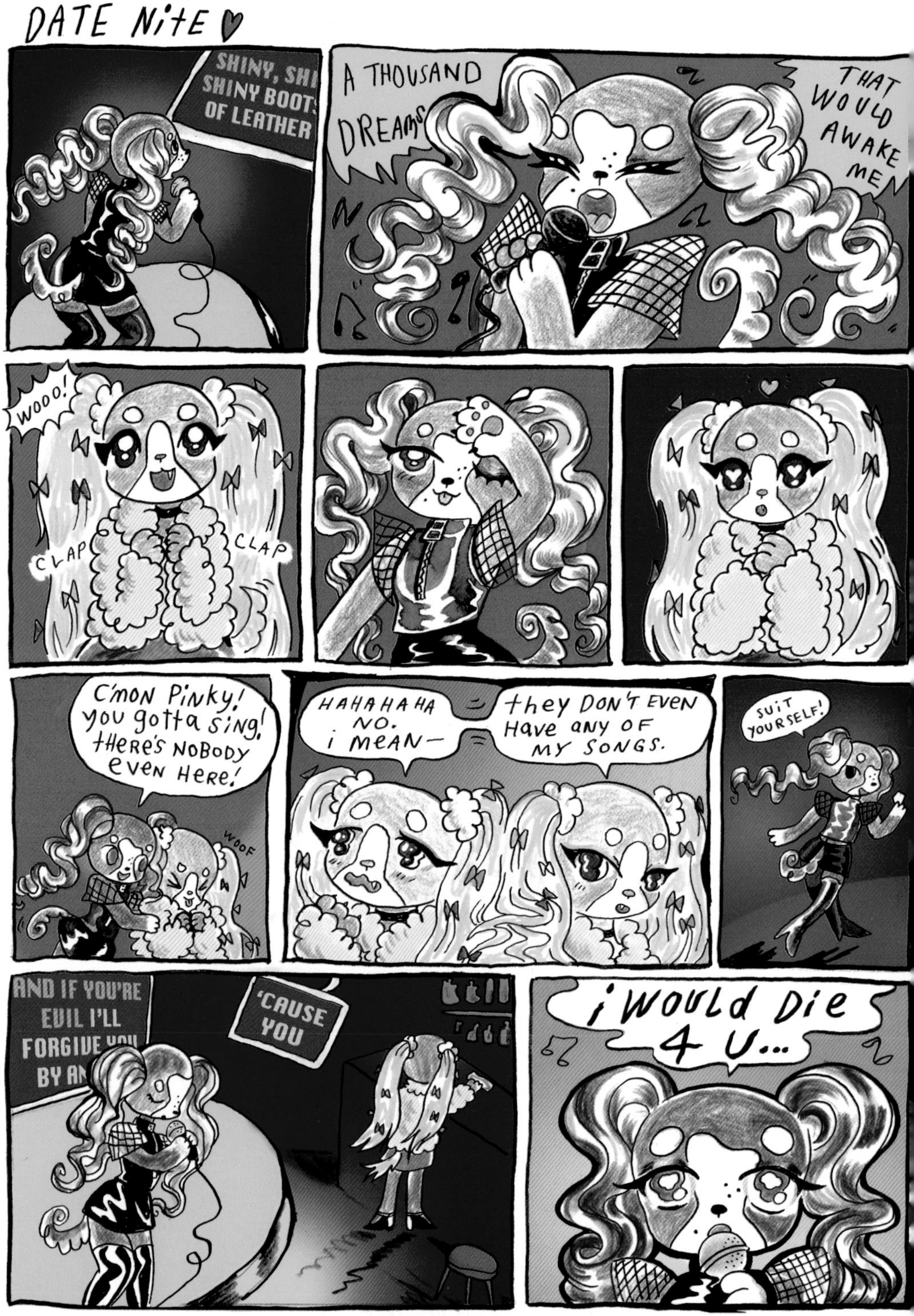
DATE Nite
SHINY, SHI
SHINY BOOTS
OF LEATHER
A THOUSAND DREAMS
THAT WOULD AWAKE ME
WOOO!
CLAP CLAP
C'MON PINKY! you gotta sing! there's NOBODY even Here!
WOOF
HAHAHAHA NO. i MEAN—
they DON'T EVEN Have any OF MY SONGS.
SUIT YOURSELF!
AND IF YOU'RE EVIL I'LL FORGIVE YOU BY AN
'CAUSE YOU
i WOULD Die 4 U...

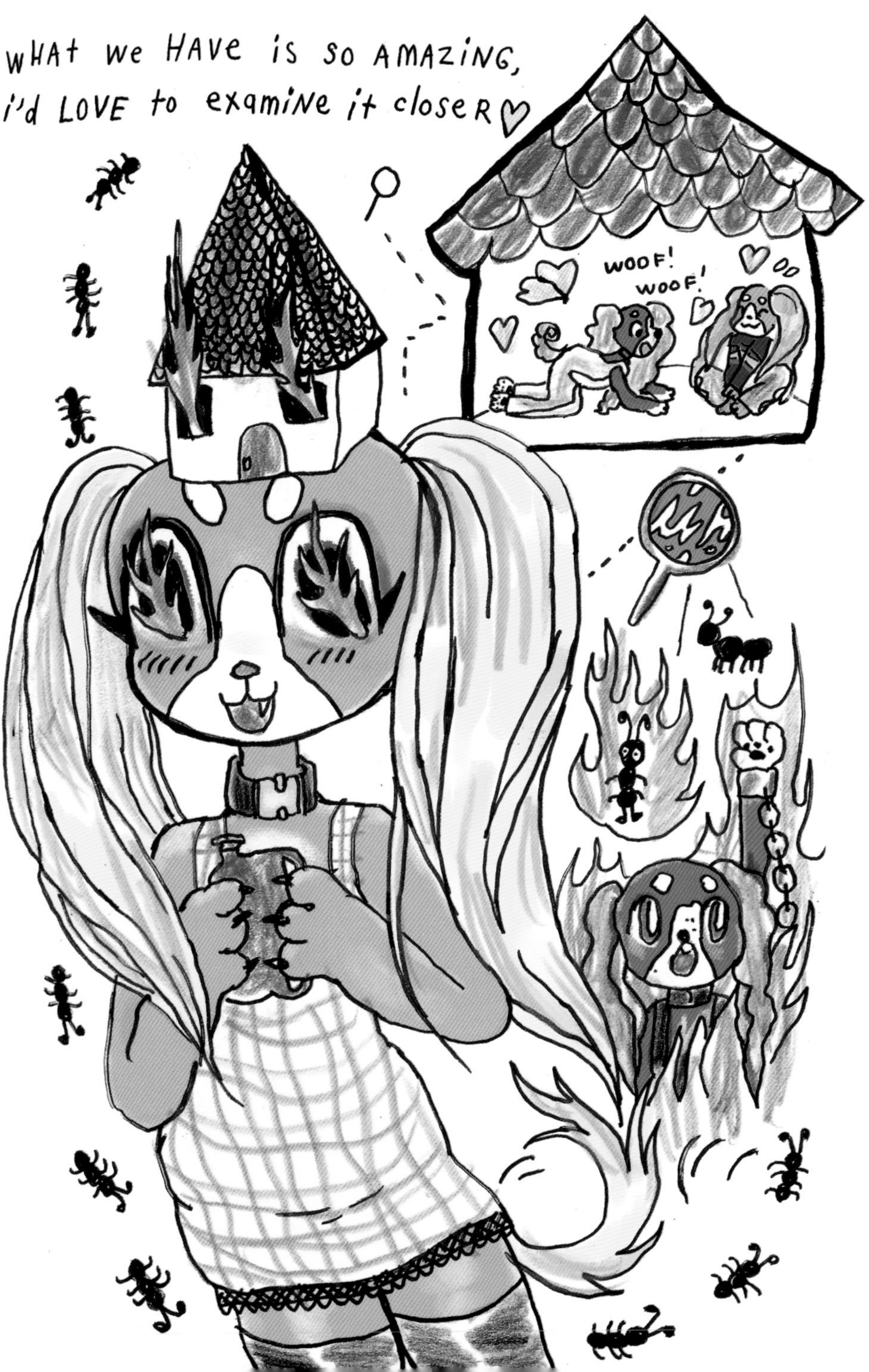
WHAT we HAVE is SO AMAZING,
i'd LOVE to examine it closer ♡
WOOF!
WOOF!

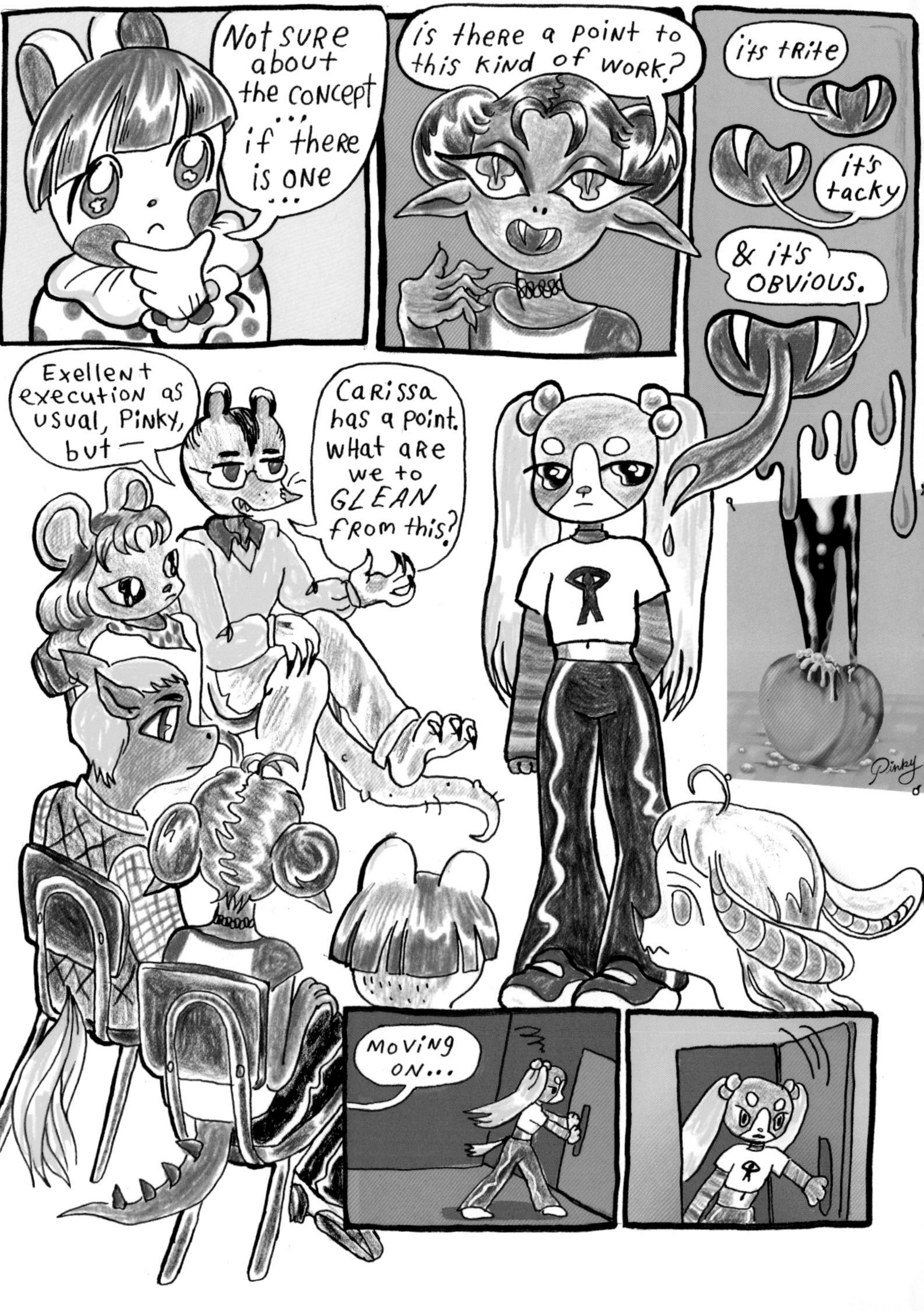
Not SURE about the concept..., if there is one...
is there a point to this kind of work?
its trite
it's tacky
& it's OBVIOUS.
Exellent execution as usual, Pinky, but—
Carissa has a point. What are we to GLEAN from this?
Pinky
MOVING ON...

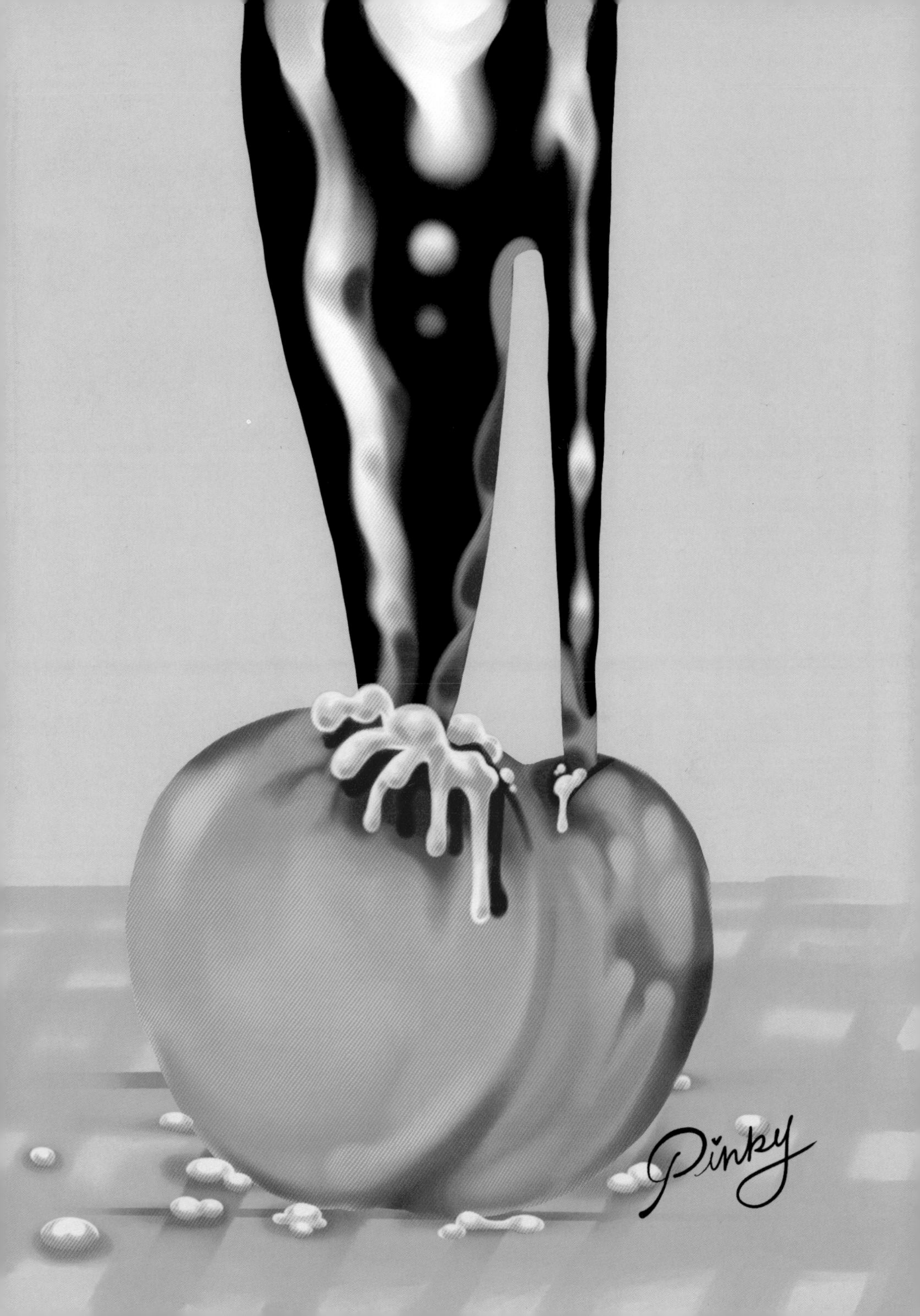
Pinky

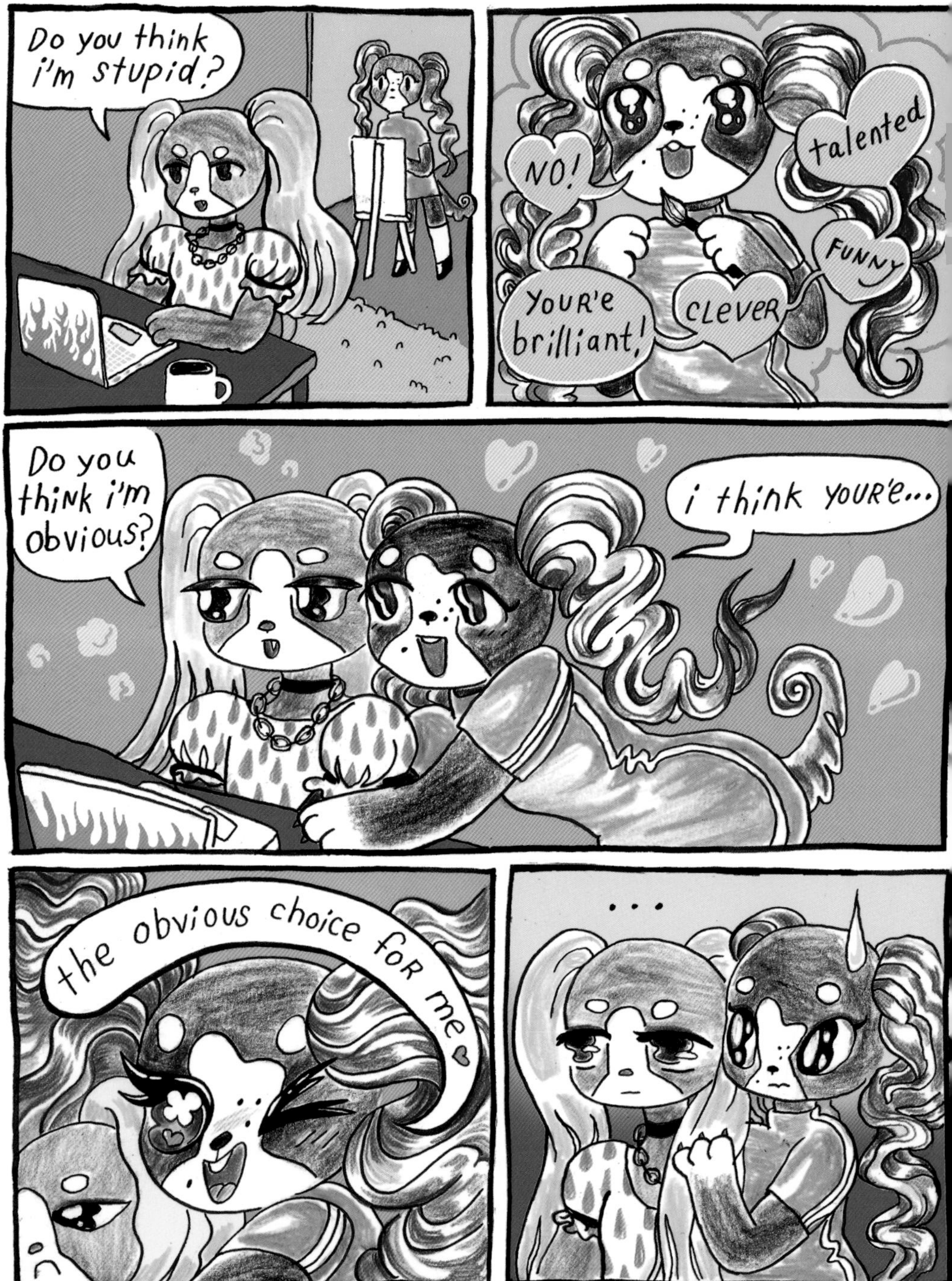

Do you think i'm stupid?
NO!
talented
FUNNY
YOUR'e brilliant!
CLEVER
Do you think i'm obvious?
i think YOUR'e...
the obvious choice FOR me
...

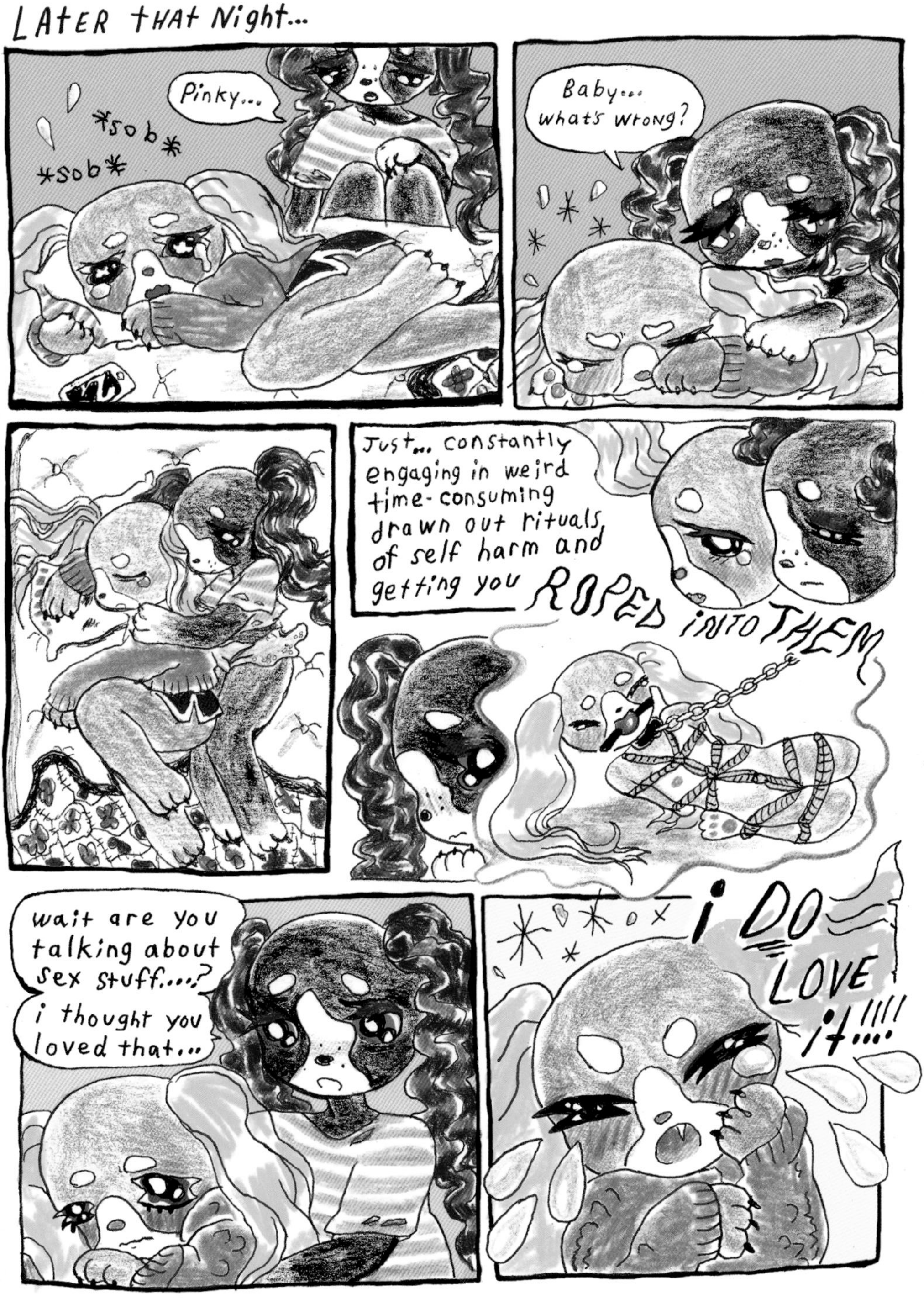
LATER that Night...
Pinky...
*sob*
*sob*
Baby... what's wrong?
Just... constantly engaging in weird time-consuming drawn out rituals of self harm and getting you ROPED INTO THEM
wait are you talking about sex stuff....?
i thought you loved that...
i DO LOVE it!!!!...

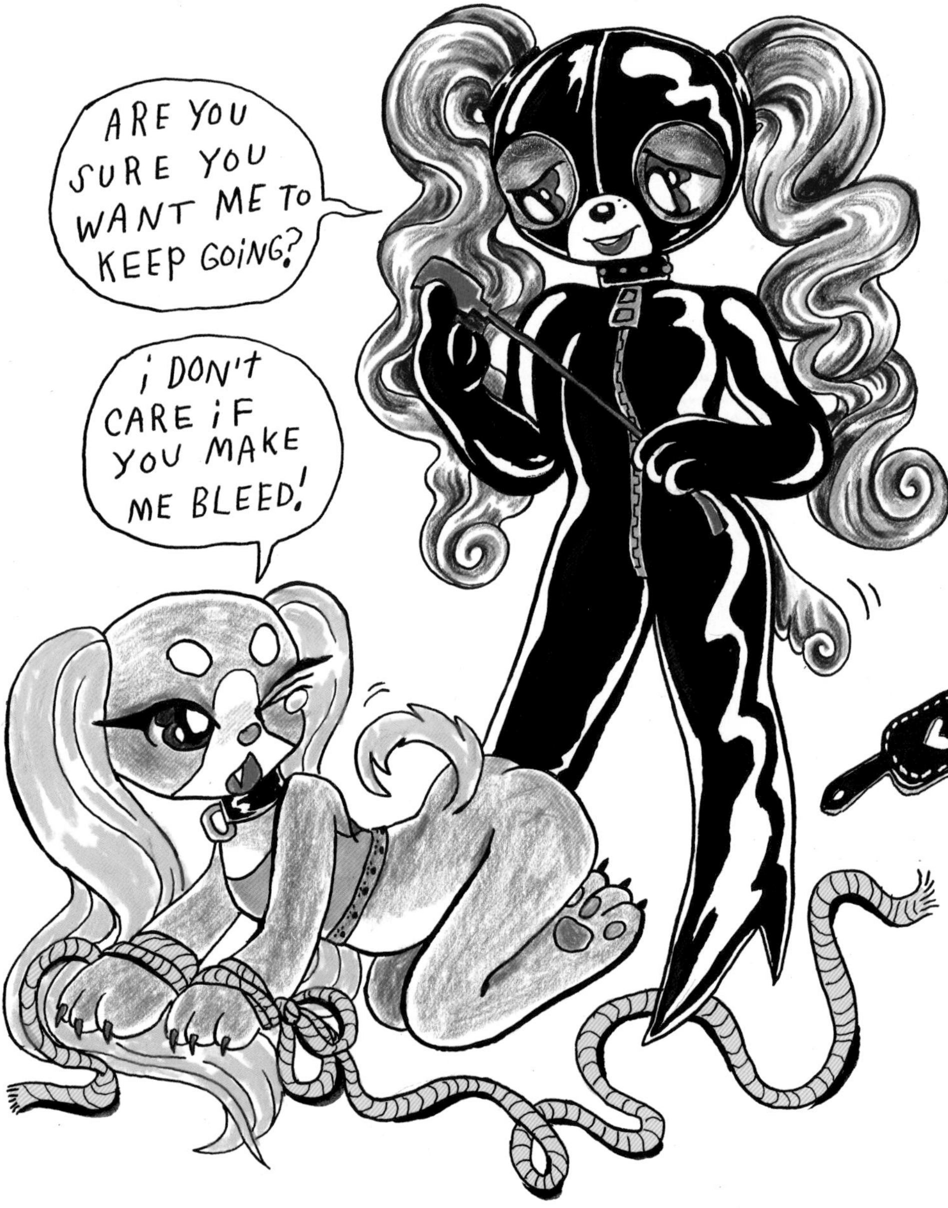
ARE YOU SURE YOU WANT ME TO KEEP GOING?
i DON'T CARE iF YOU MAKE ME BLEED!

i GUESS
WE NEVER REALLY TALKED
ABOUT OUR PASTS

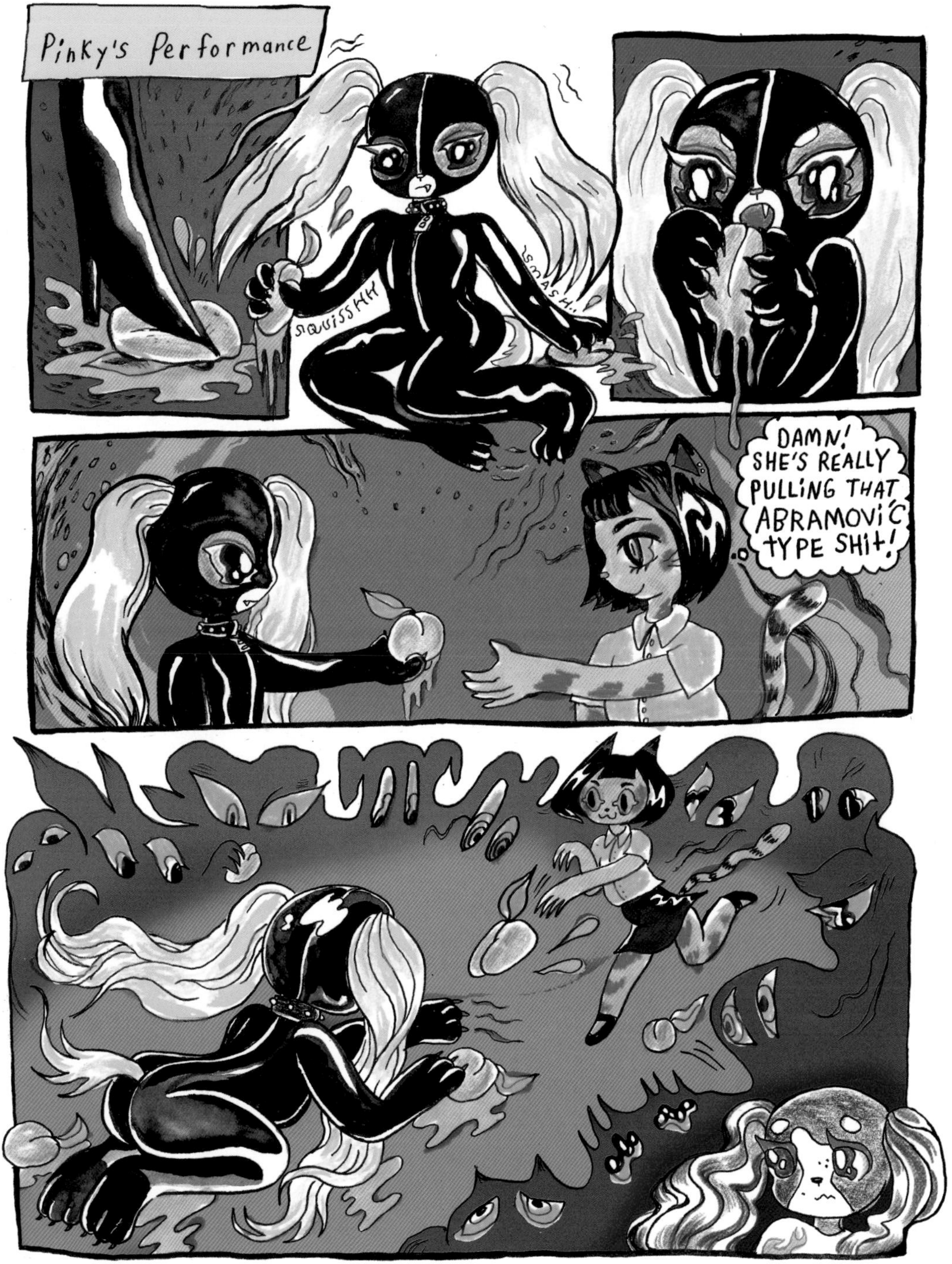
Pinky's Performance
SQUISSHH
SMASH!
DAMN! SHE'S REALLY PULLING THAT ABRAMOVIĆ TYPE SHIT!

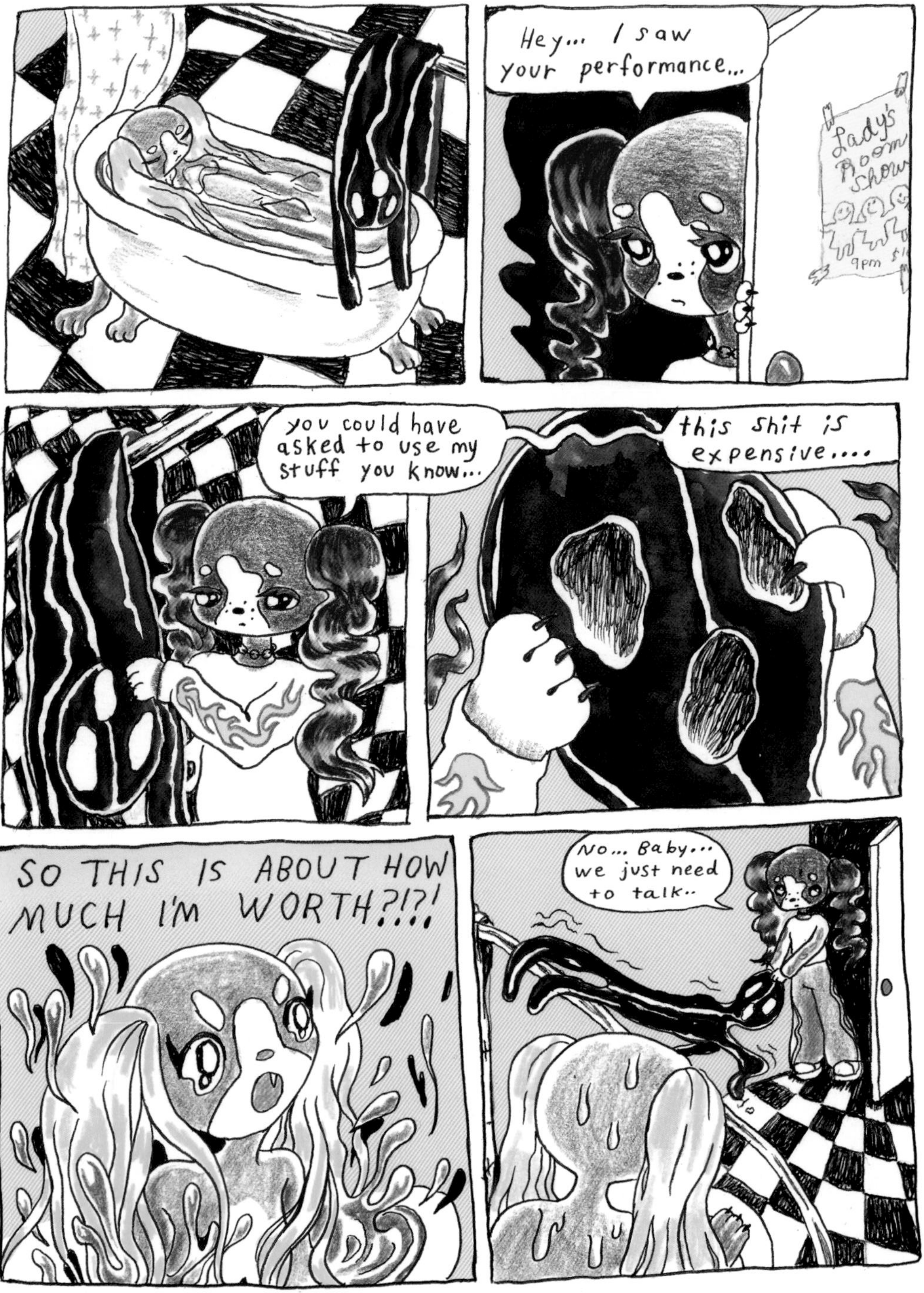
Hey... I saw your performance...
Lady's Room Show
9pm
you could have asked to use my stuff you know...
this shit is expensive....
SO THIS IS ABOUT HOW MUCH I'M WORTH?!?!
No... Baby... we just need to talk..

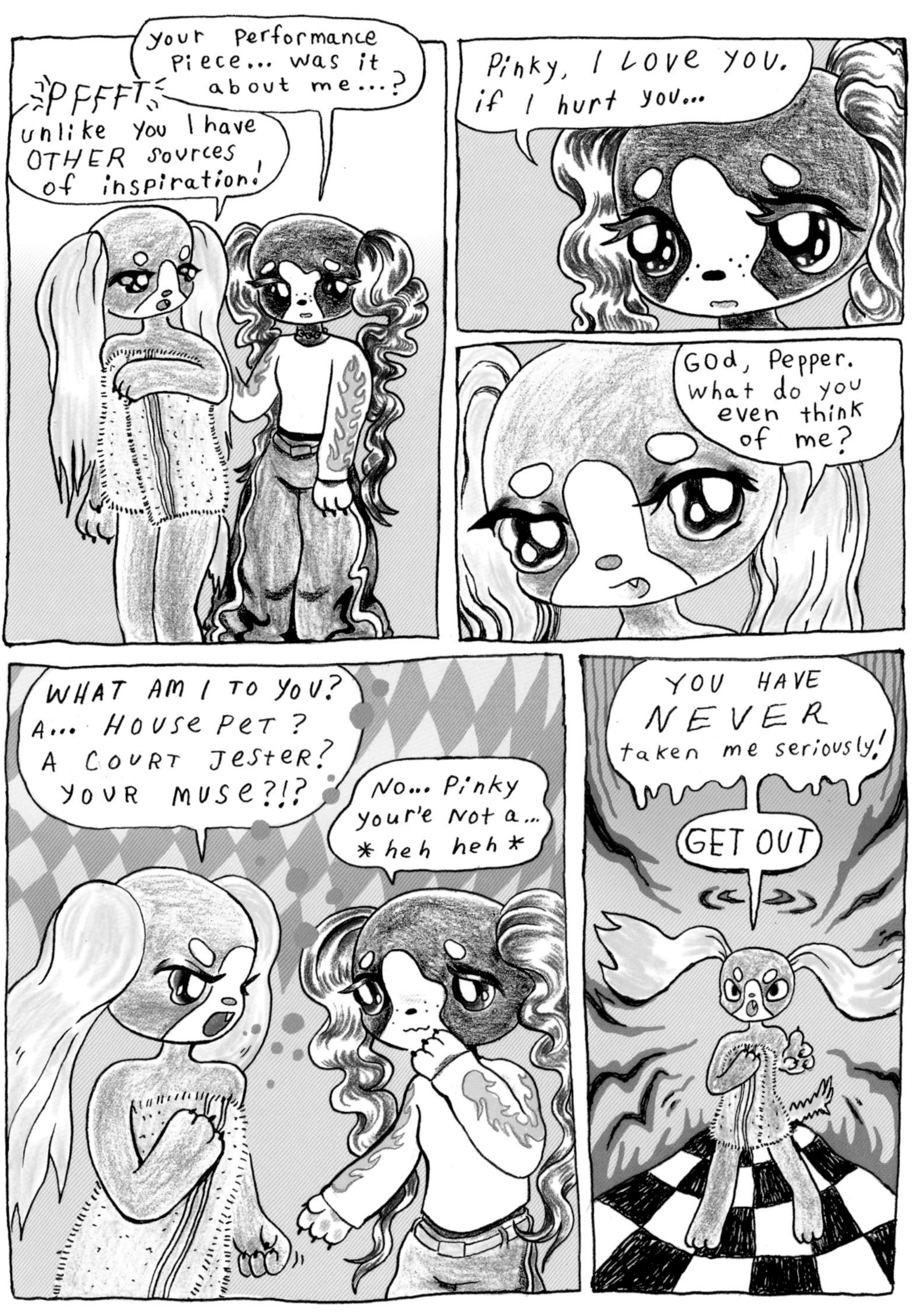

your performance piece... was it about me...?
PFFFT
unlike you I have OTHER sources of inspiration!
Pinky, I LOVE YOU. if I hurt you...
GOd, Pepper. what do you even think of me?
WHAT AM I TO YOU? A... HOUSE PET? A COURT JESTER? YOUR MUSE?!?
No... Pinky your'e Not a... *heh heh*
YOU HAVE NEVER taken me seriously!
GET OUT

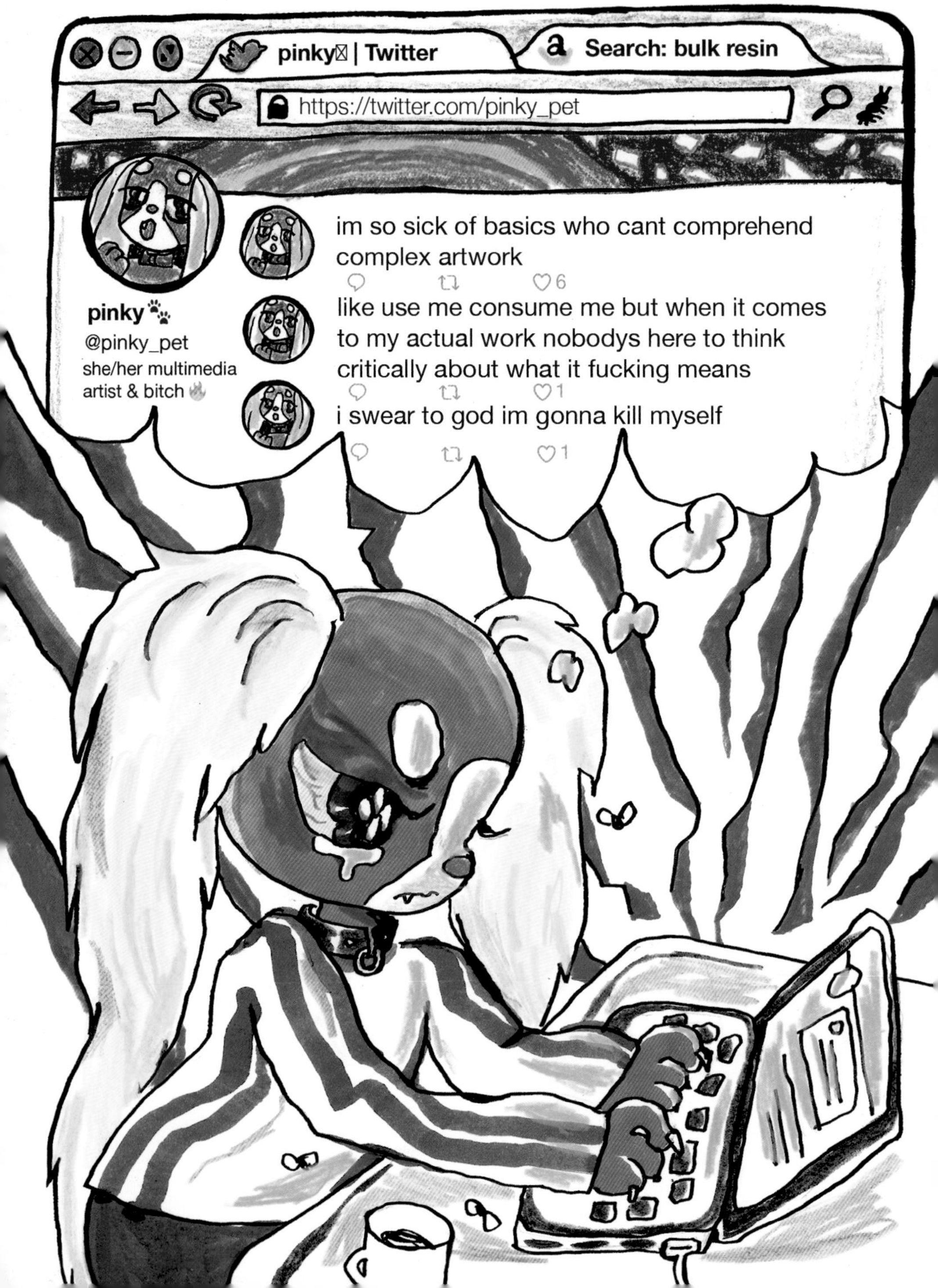

pinky | Twitter
Search: bulk resin
https://twitter.com/pinky_pet
pinky
@pinky_pet
she/her multimedia artist & bitch
im so sick of basics who cant comprehend complex artwork
6
like use me consume me but when it comes to my actual work nobodys here to think critically about what it fucking means
1
i swear to god im gonna kill myself
1

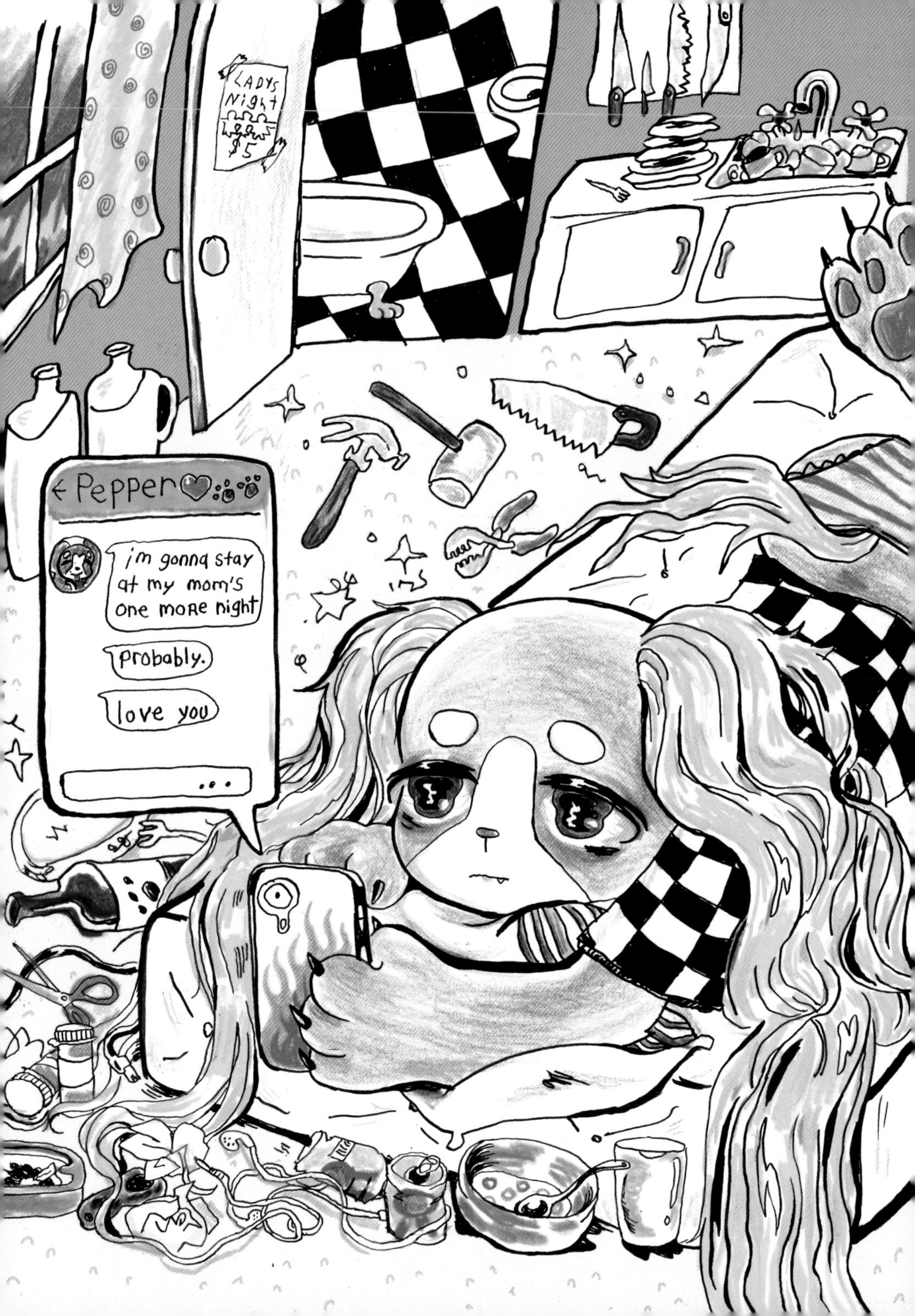
LADYS Night $5
Pepper
im gonna stay at my mom's one more night
probably.
love you

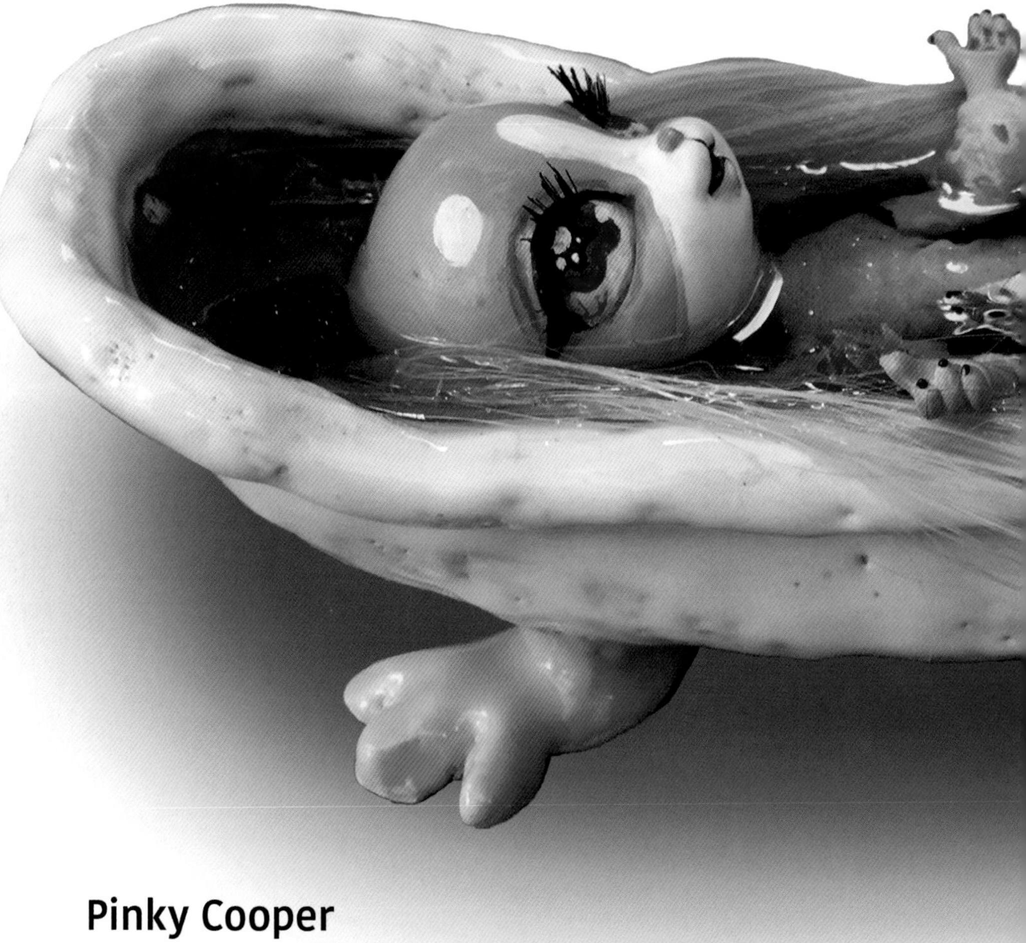

**Pinky Cooper**
*Final Piece* (2018)
Body and resin in bathtub

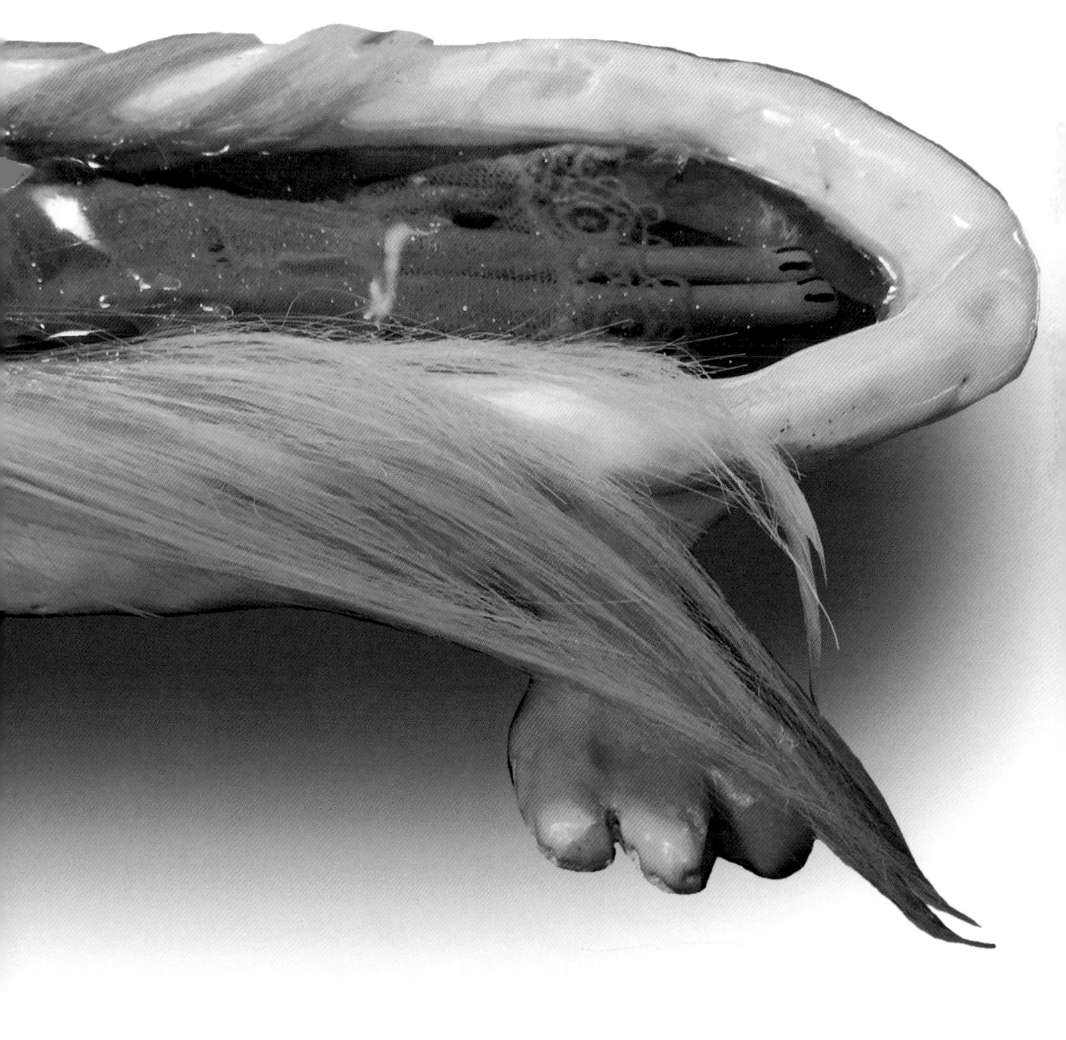

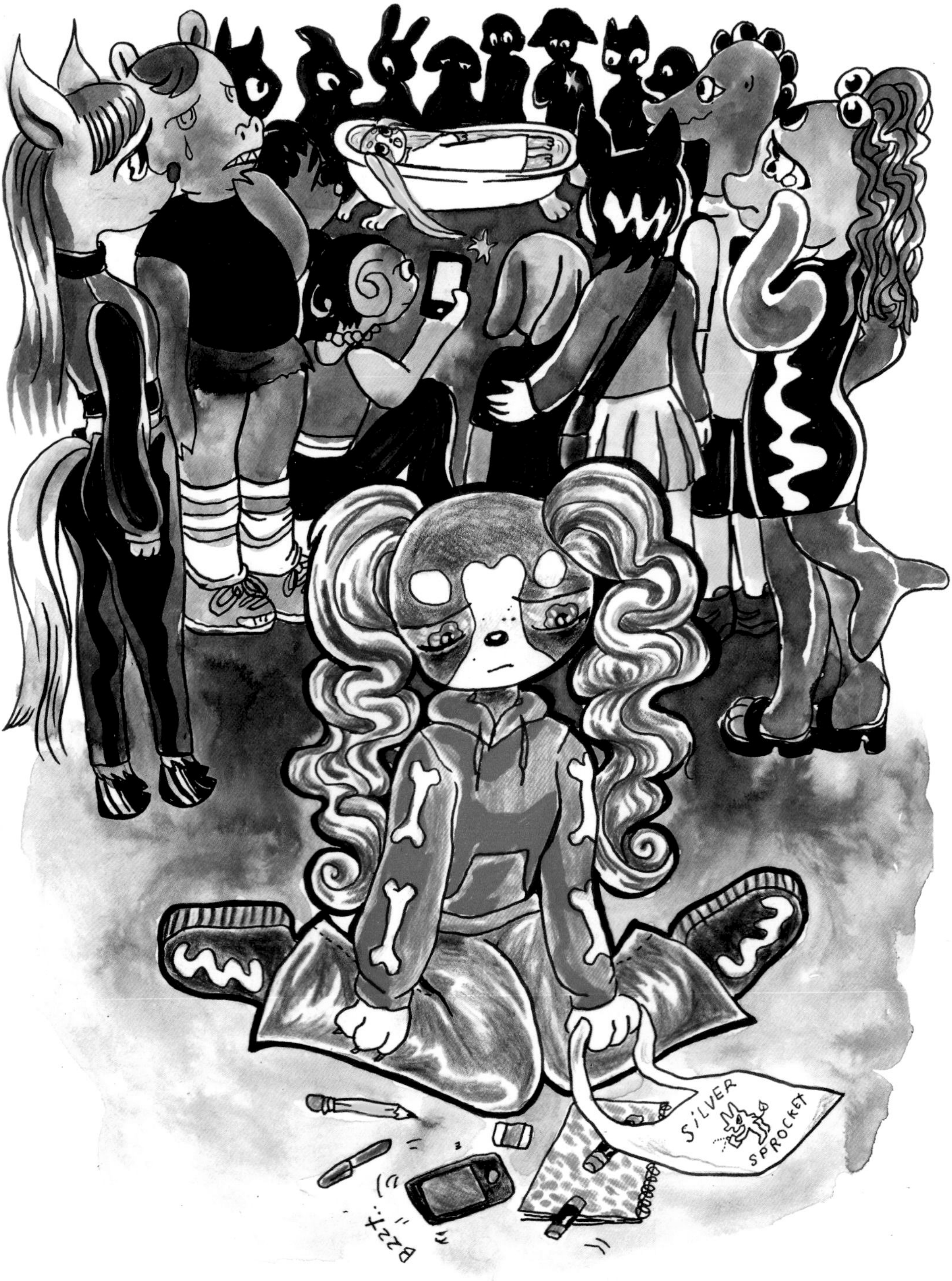
SILVER SPROCKET
BZZT..

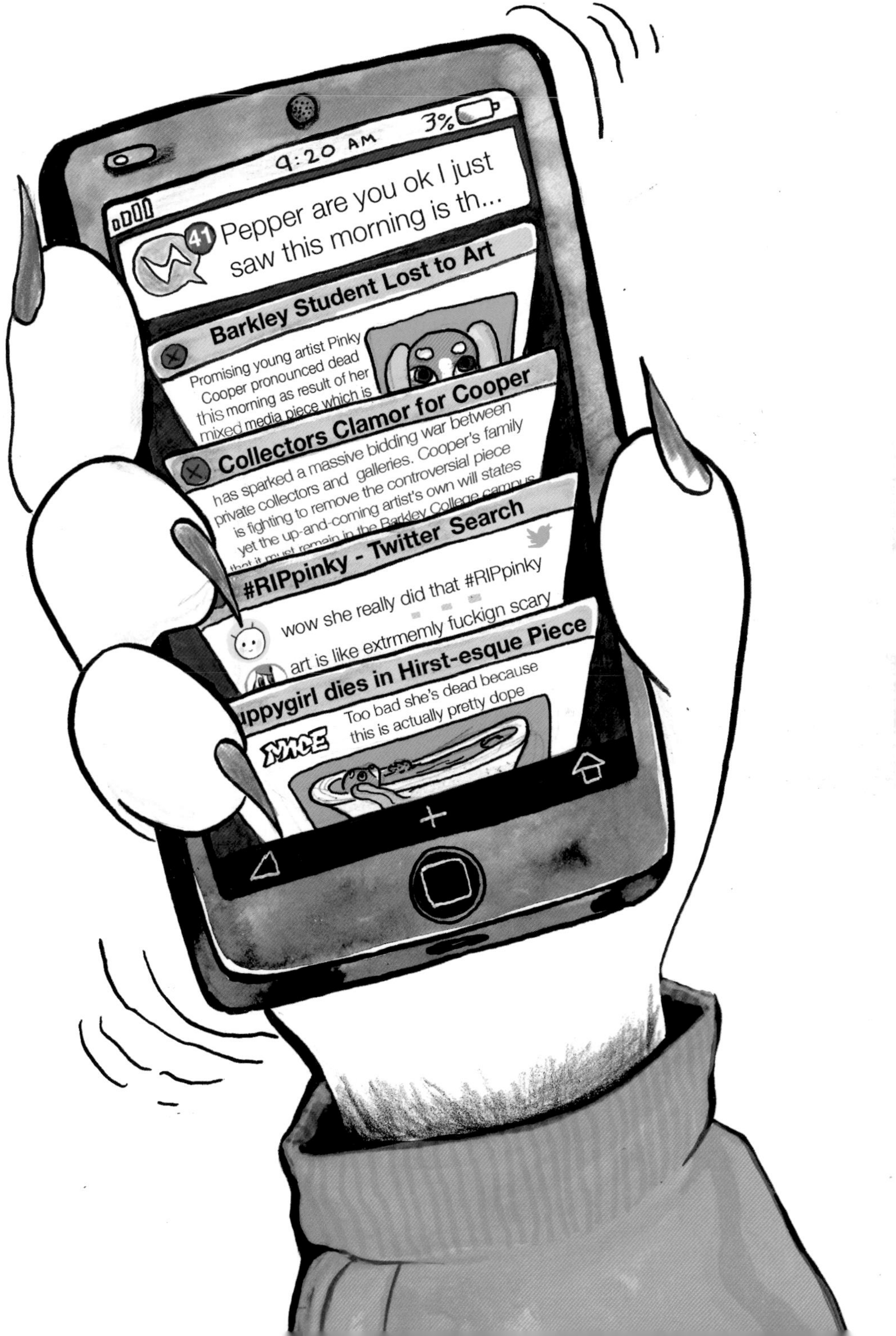

9:20 AM
3%
41
Pepper are you ok I just saw this morning is th...
Barkley Student Lost to Art
Promising young artist Pinky Cooper pronounced dead this morning as result of her mixed media piece which is
Collectors Clamor for Cooper
has sparked a massive bidding war between private collectors and galleries. Cooper's family is fighting to remove the controversial piece yet the up-and-coming artist's own will states
#RIPpinky - Twitter Search
#RIPpinky
wow she really did that #RIPpinky
art is like extrmemly fuckign scary
uppygirl dies in Hirst-esque Piece
Too bad she's dead because this is actually pretty dope

She's GONE.

i CAN't go to SCHOOL ANYMORE.
EVERY DAY is LikE A FUNERAL.

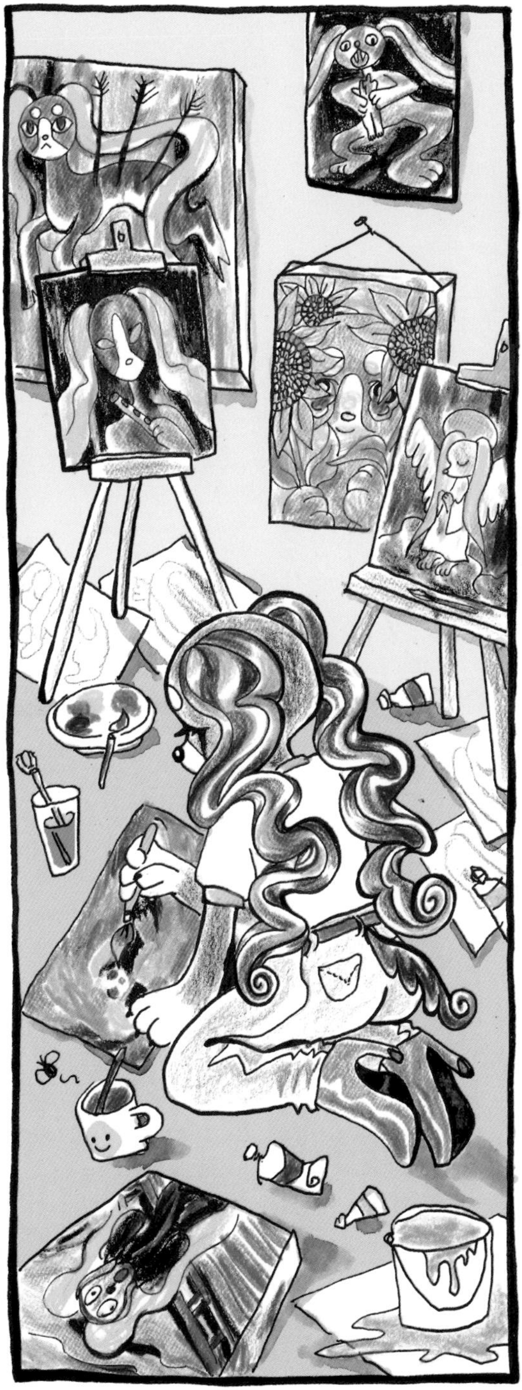
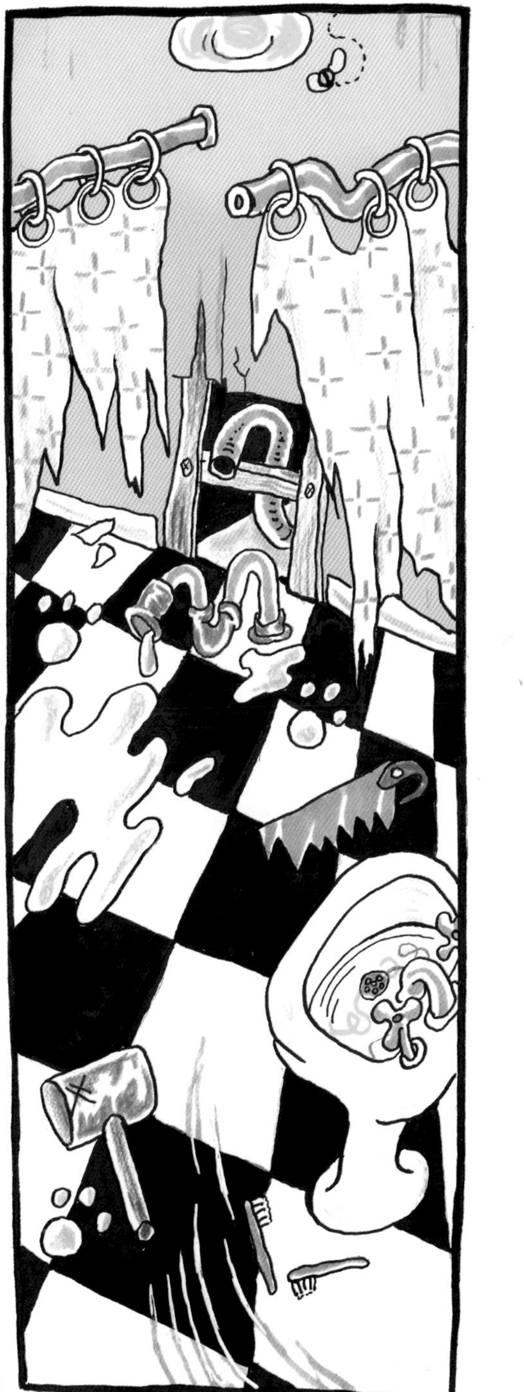

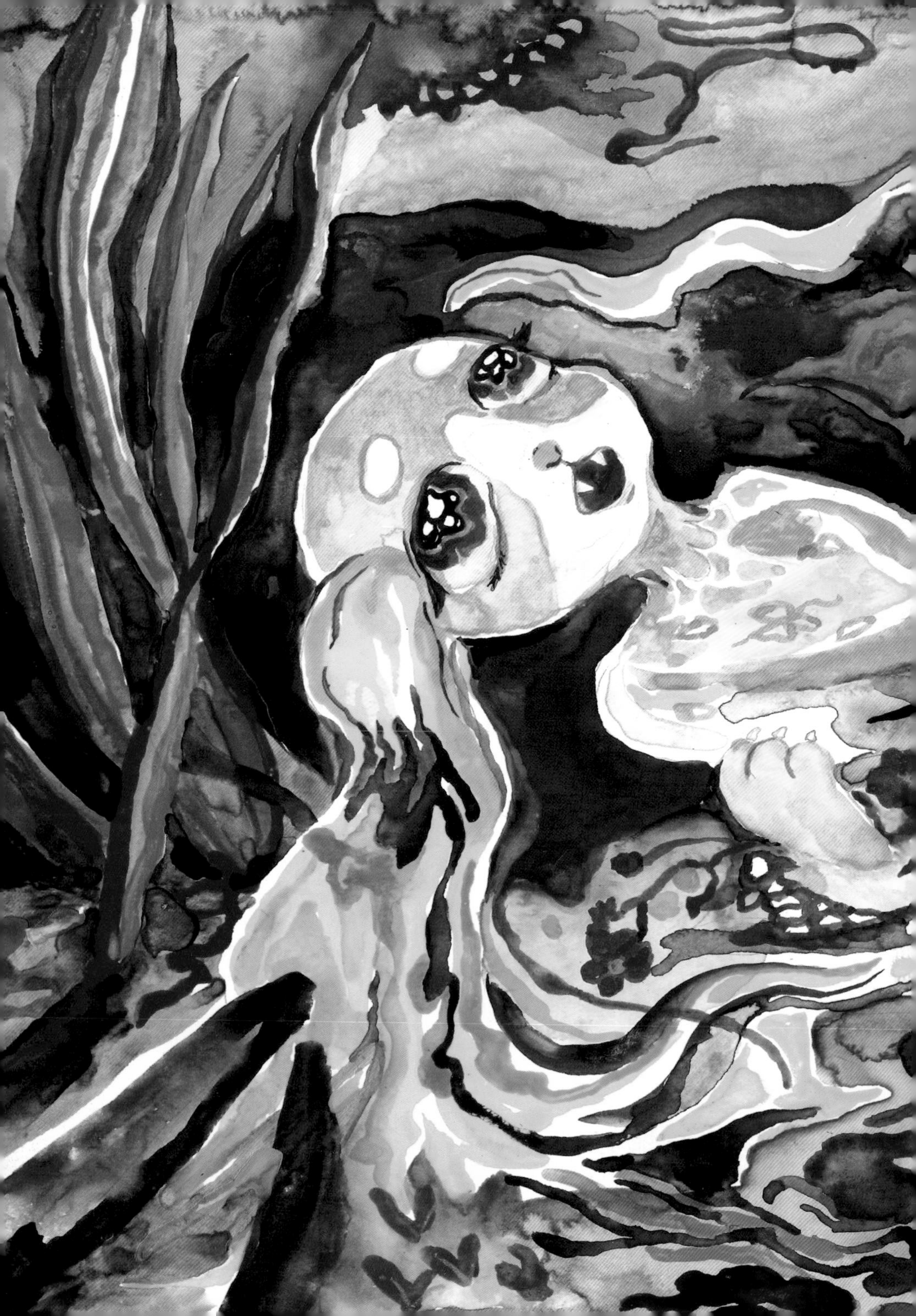

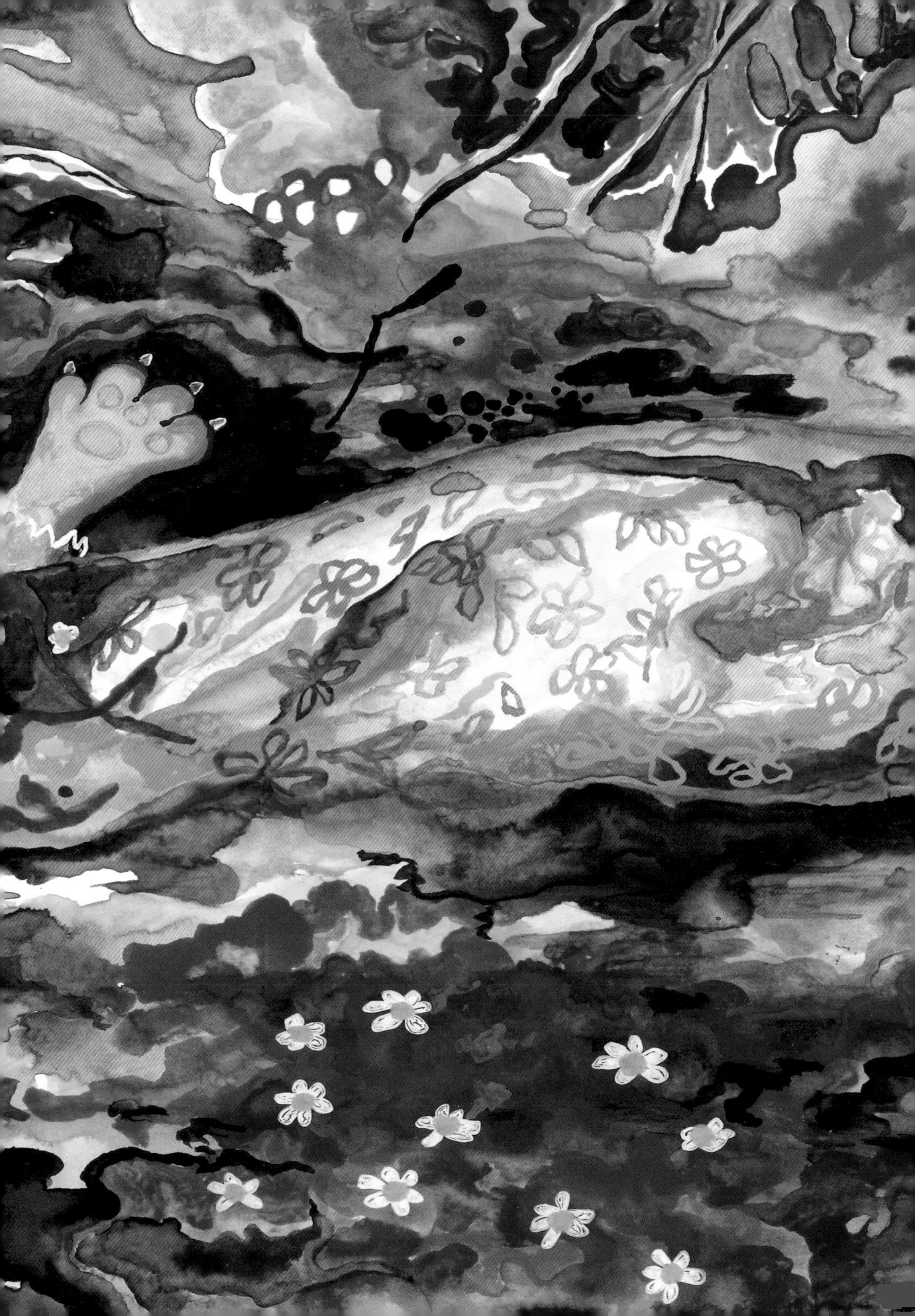

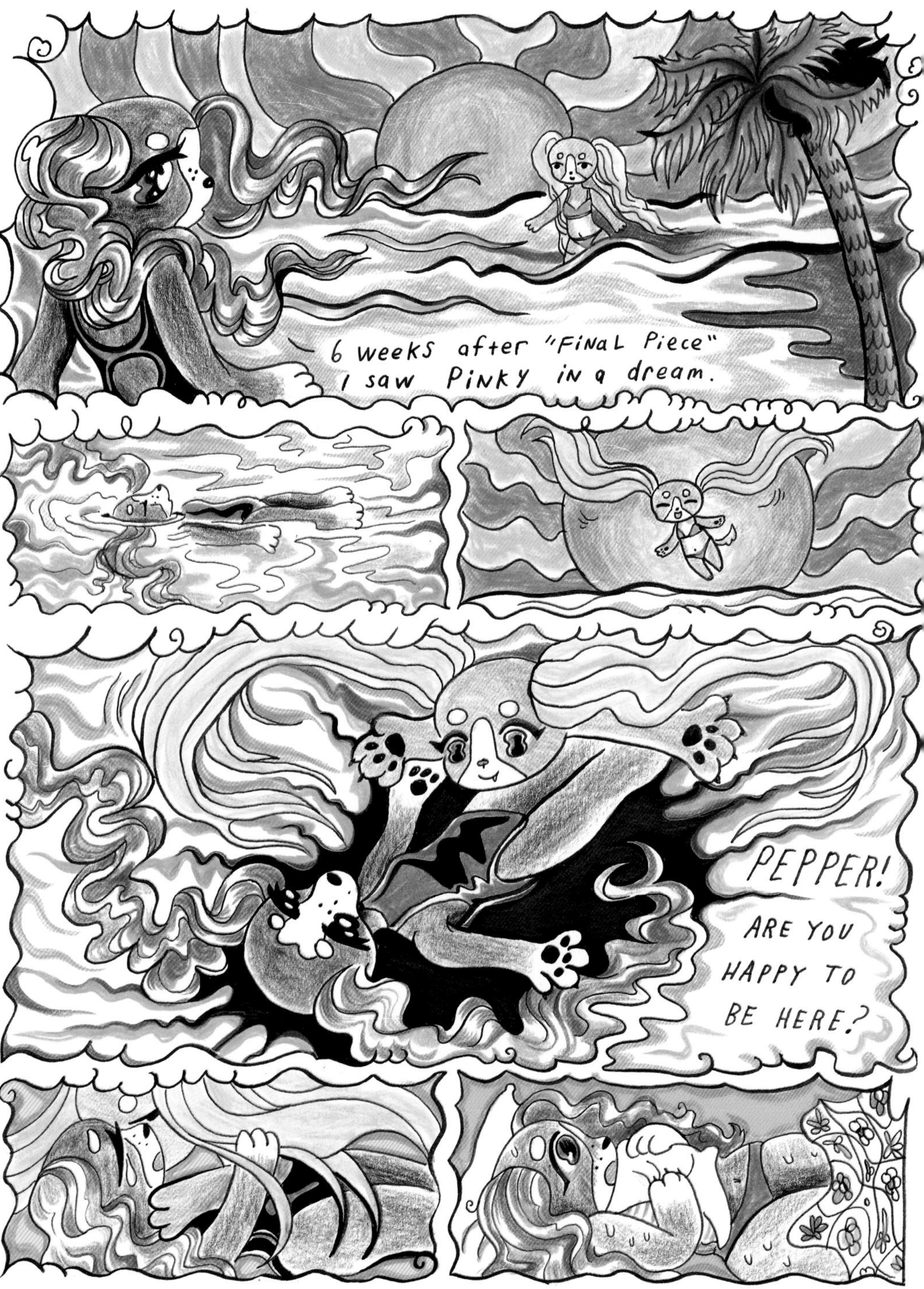
6 weeks after "Final Piece"
I saw Pinky in a dream.
PEPPER!
ARE YOU HAPPY TO BE HERE?

SHHH, DON'T EVEN WORRY♡
it DOSEN't FEEL LiKE ANYThiNG!

OUR father aRt iN heaveN
aRt iN heaveN iN heaveN
HOLY mother if i die
befoRe i wake ; pray
for us siNNers at the
hOUR of OUR death and
forgive me PiNKY PiNKY
PiNKY PiNKY

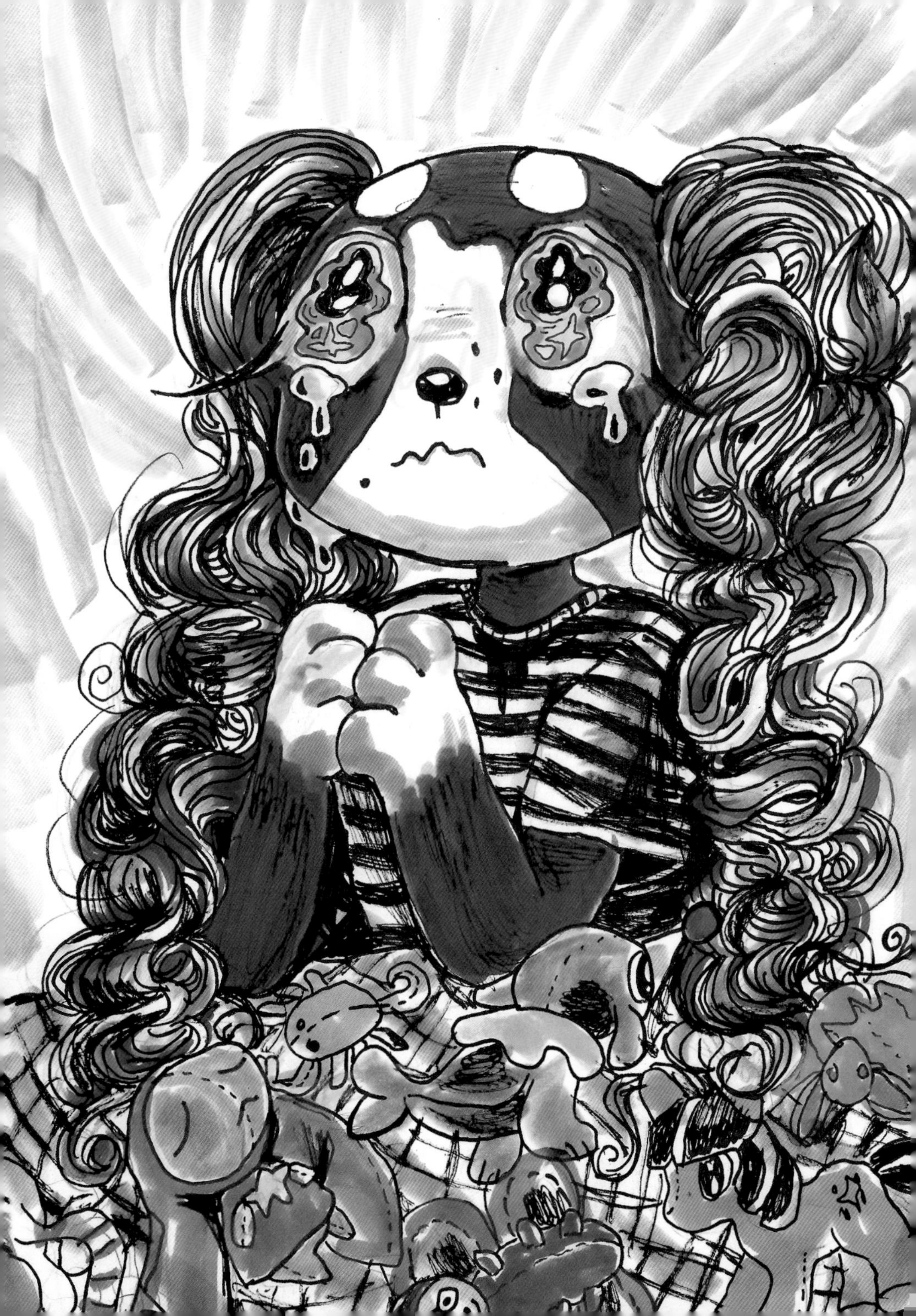

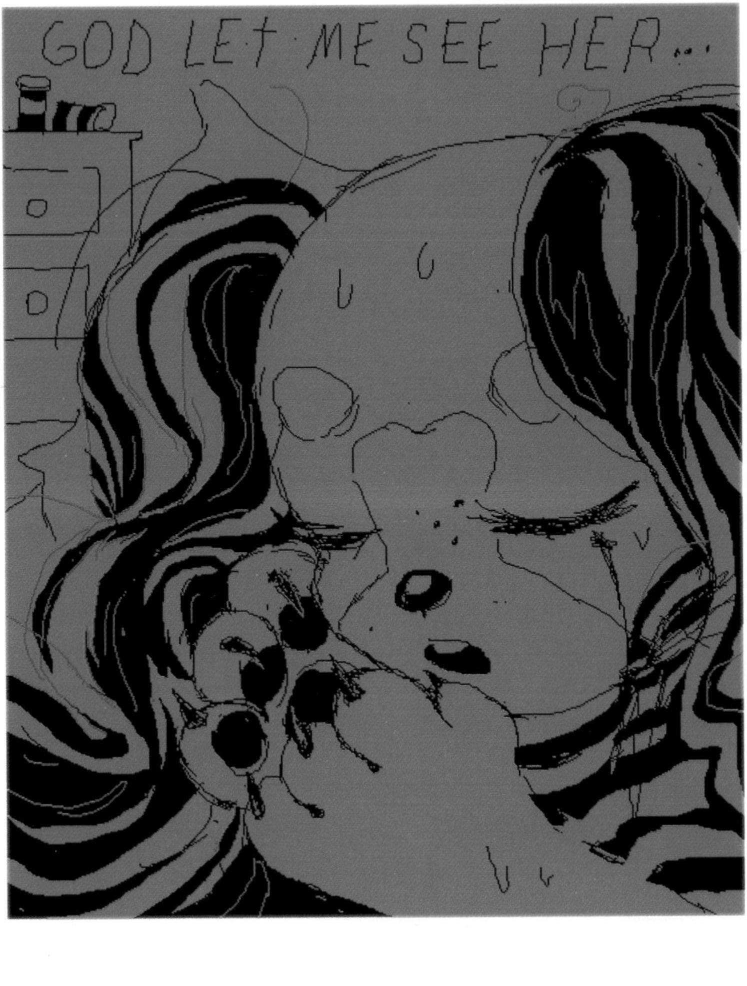
GOD LET ME SEE HER...

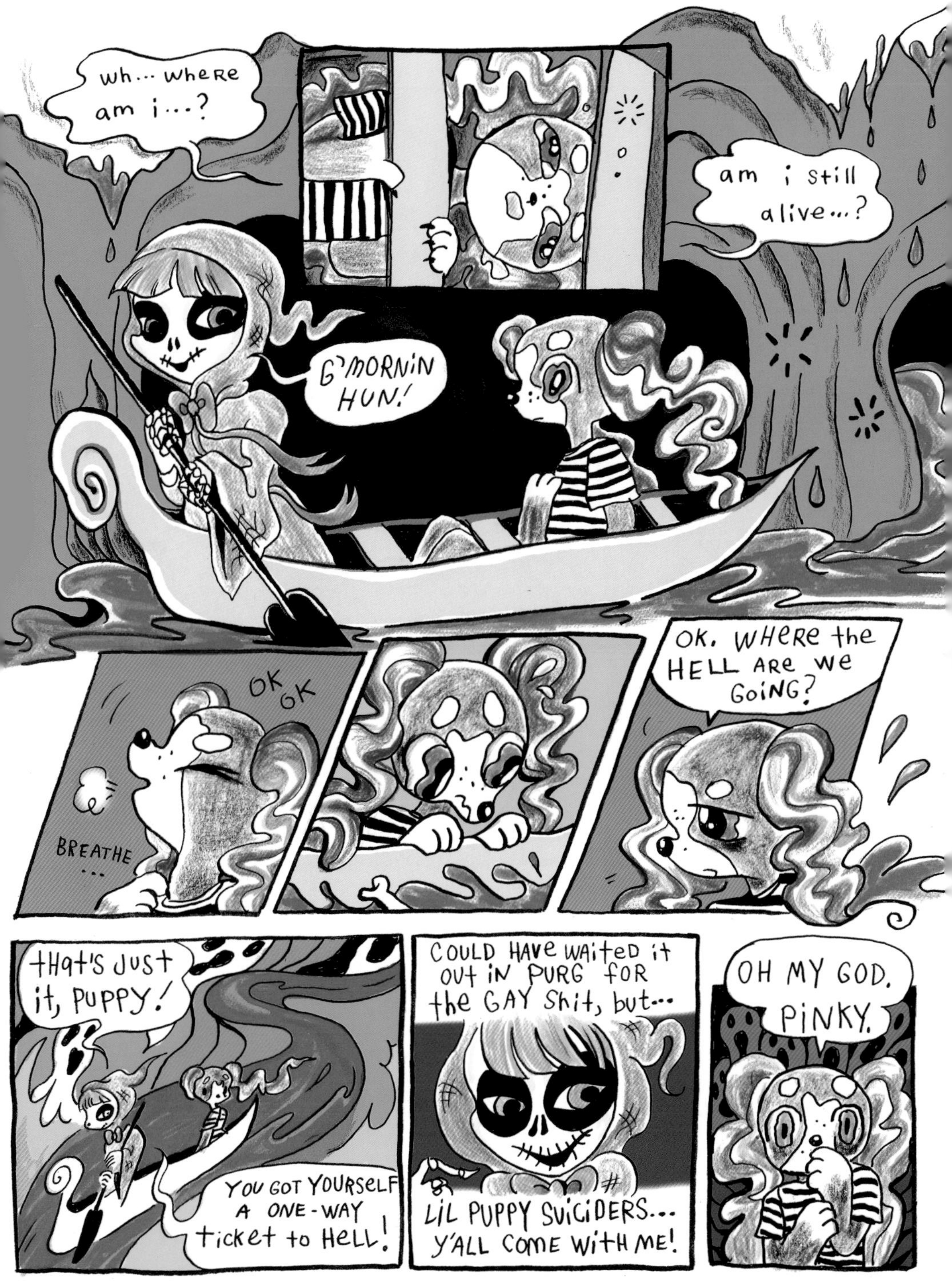

wh... where am i...?
am i still alive...?
G'MORNIN HUN!
OK OK
BREATHE...
OK. WHERE the HELL ARE WE GOING?
that's just it, PUPPY!
YOU GOT YOURSELF A ONE-WAY ticket to HELL!
COULD HAVE WAITED it out in PURG for the GAY Shit, but...
LIL PUPPY SUICIDERS... Y'ALL COME WITH ME!
OH MY GOD. PINKY.

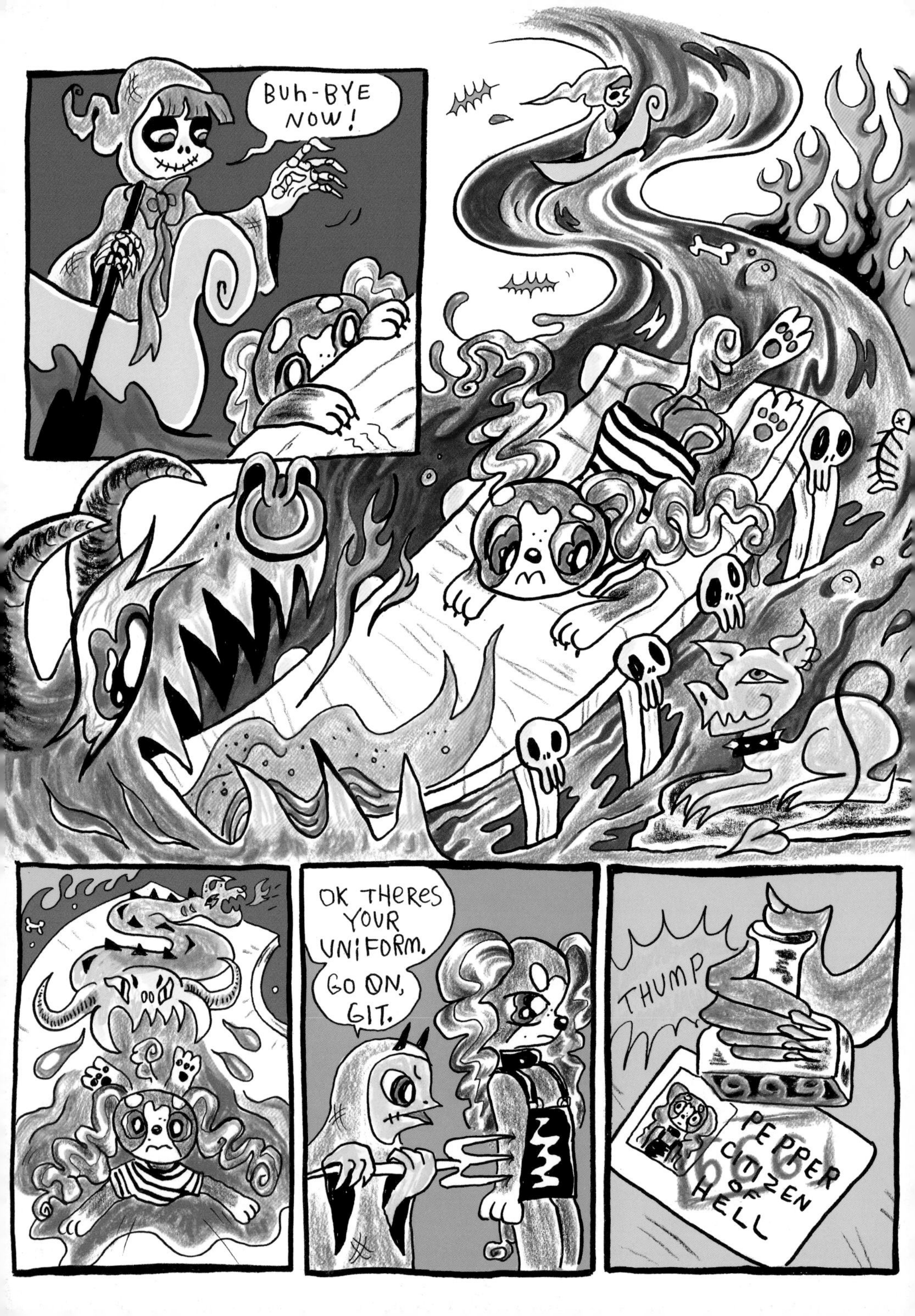
BUH-BYE NOW!
OK THERES YOUR UNIFORM.
GO ON, GIT.
THUMP
666
PEPPER CITIZEN OF HELL

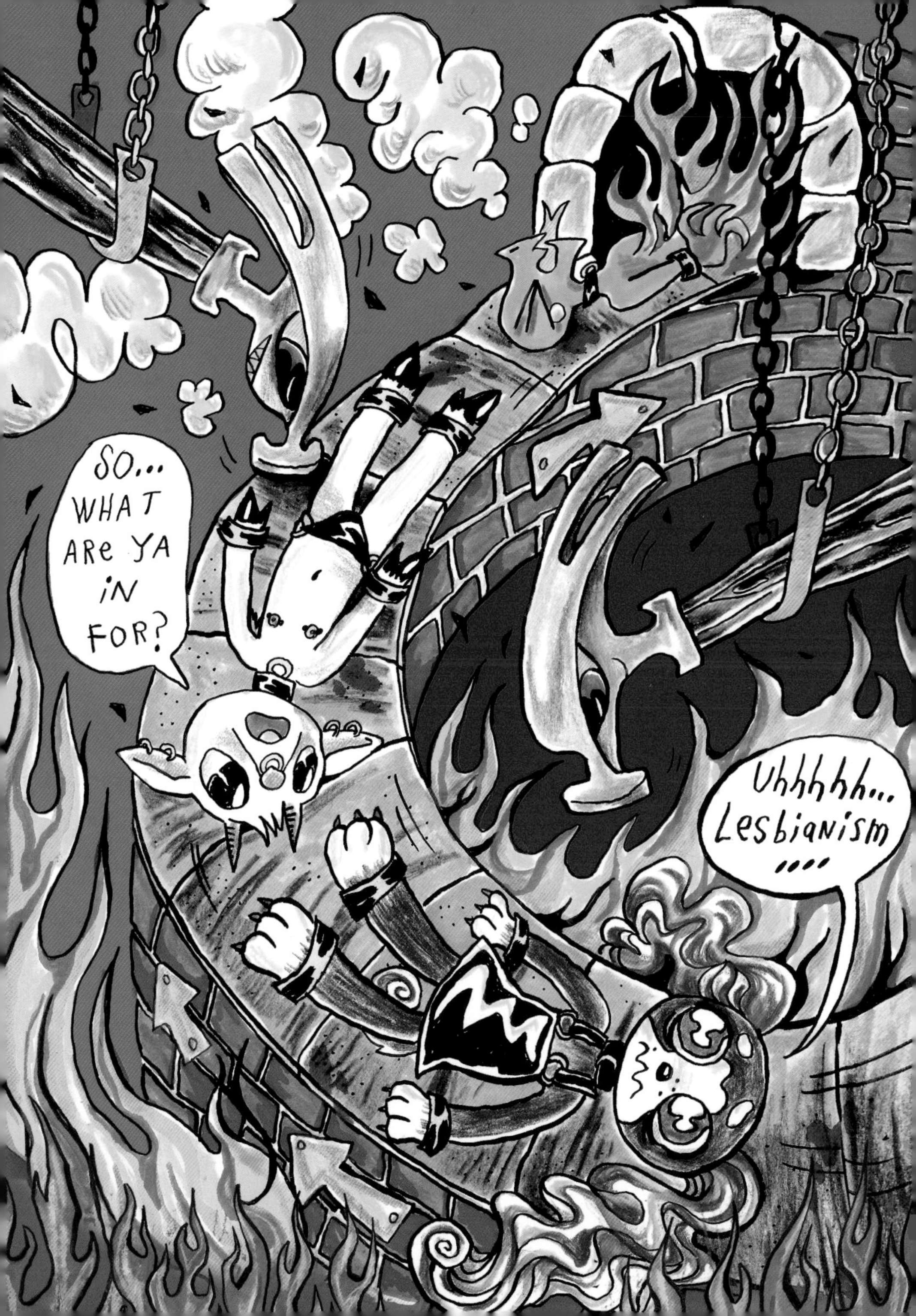
SO... WHAT ARE YA IN FOR?
Uhhhhh... Lesbianism....

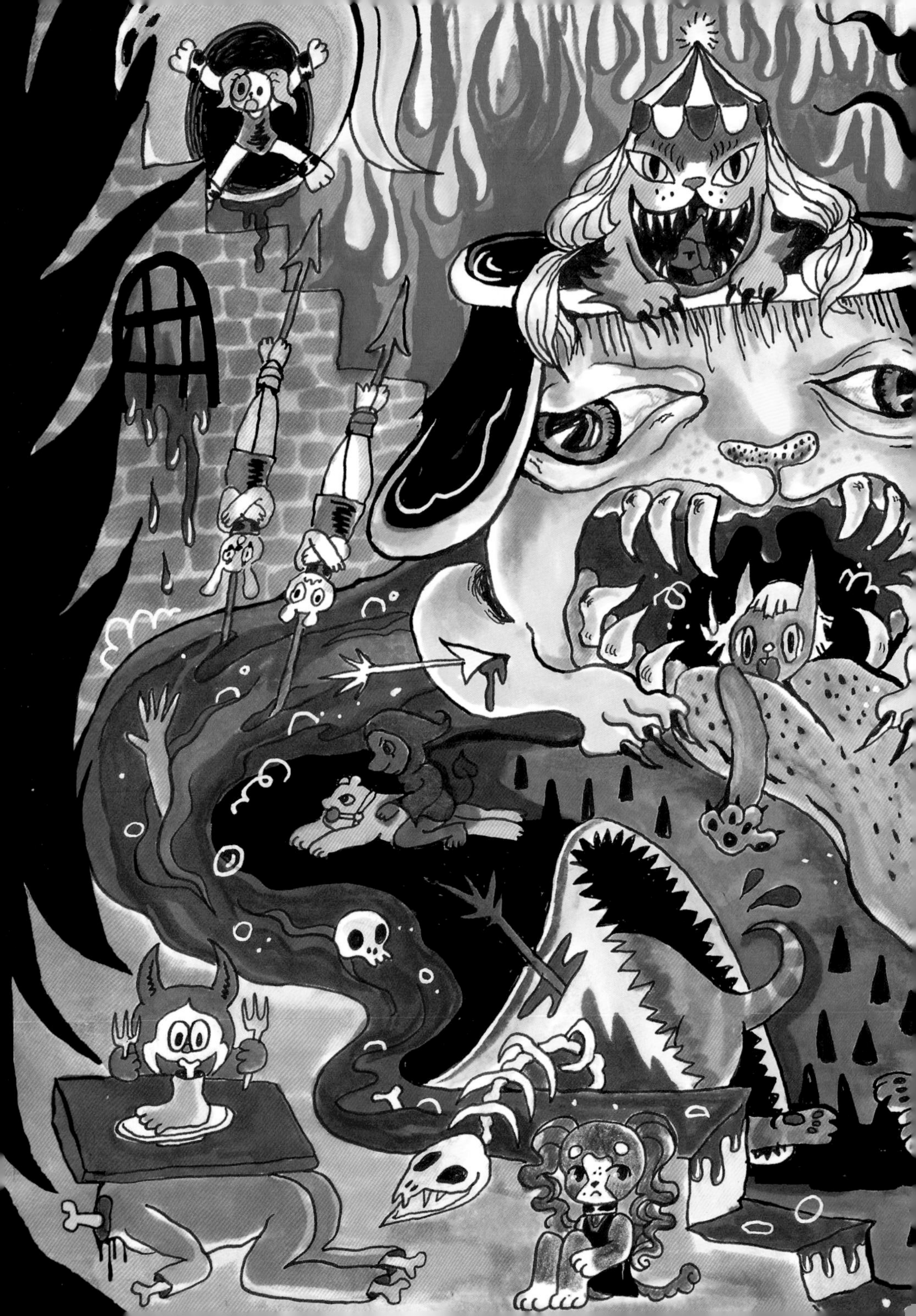

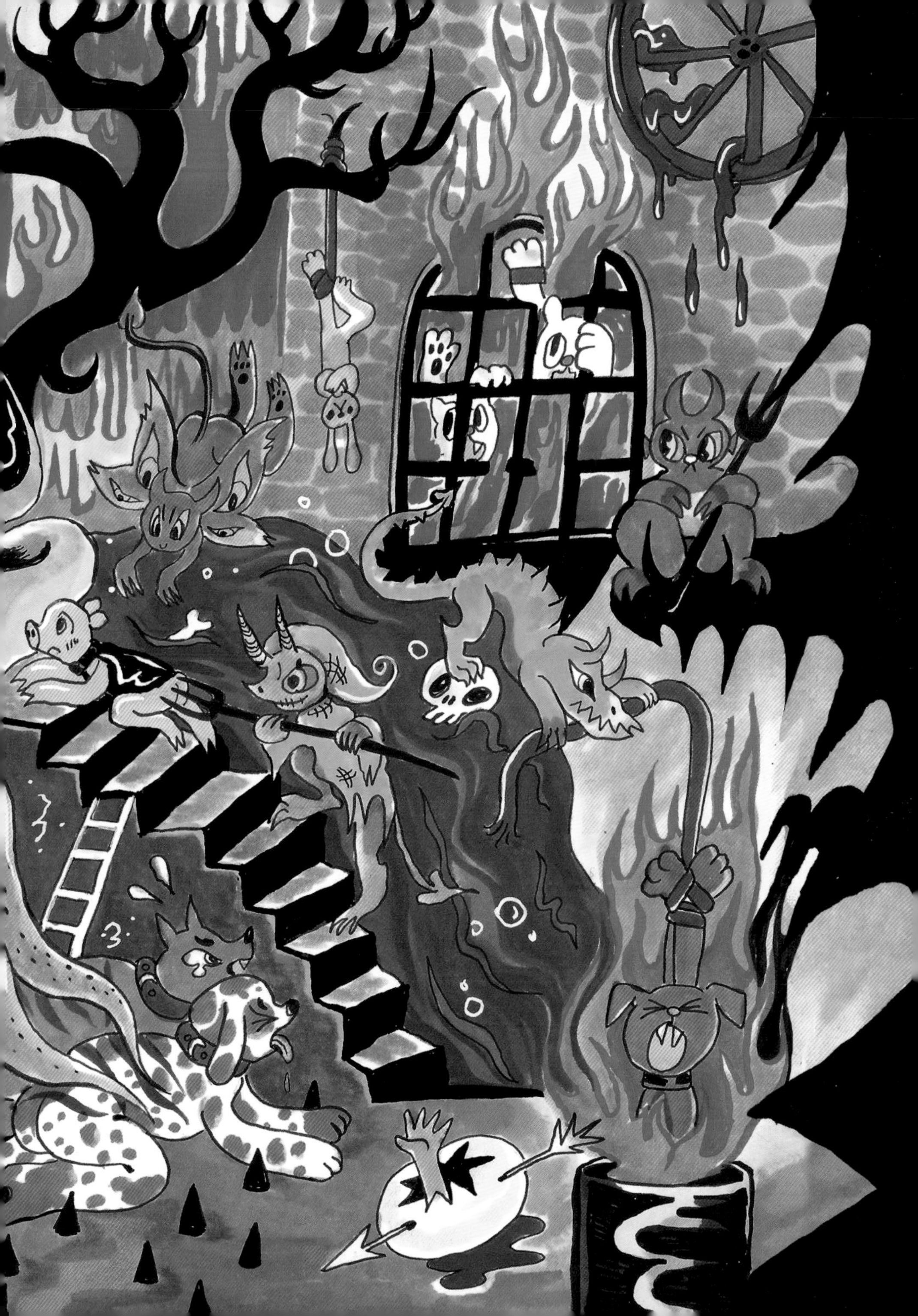

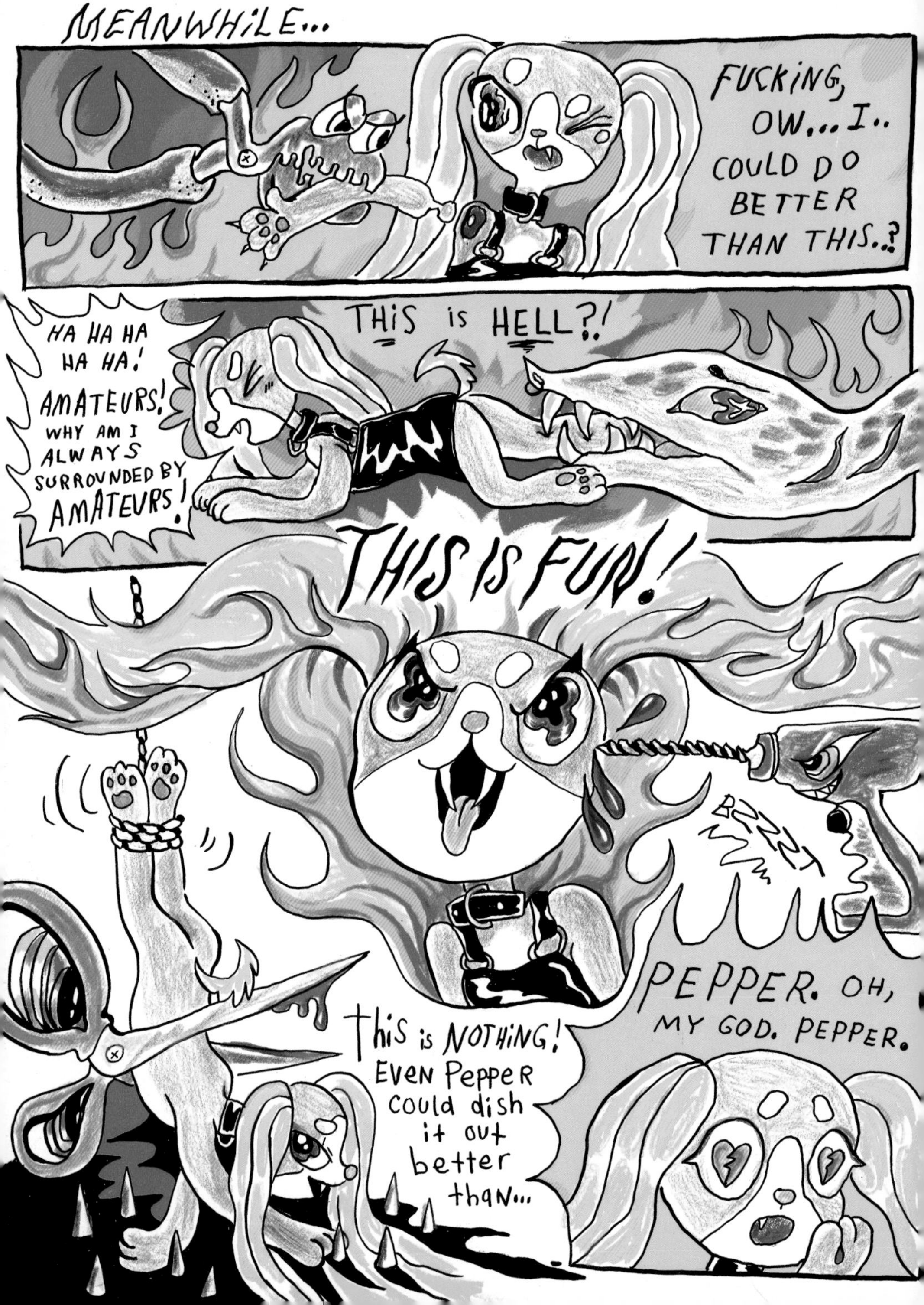
MEANWHILE...
FUCKING, OW... I.. COULD DO BETTER THAN THIS..?
HA HA HA HA HA! AMATEURS! WHY AM I ALWAYS SURROUNDED BY AMATEURS!
THIS is HELL?!
THIS IS FUN!
BZZZT
This is NOTHING! Even Pepper could dish it out better than...
PEPPER. OH, MY GOD. PEPPER.

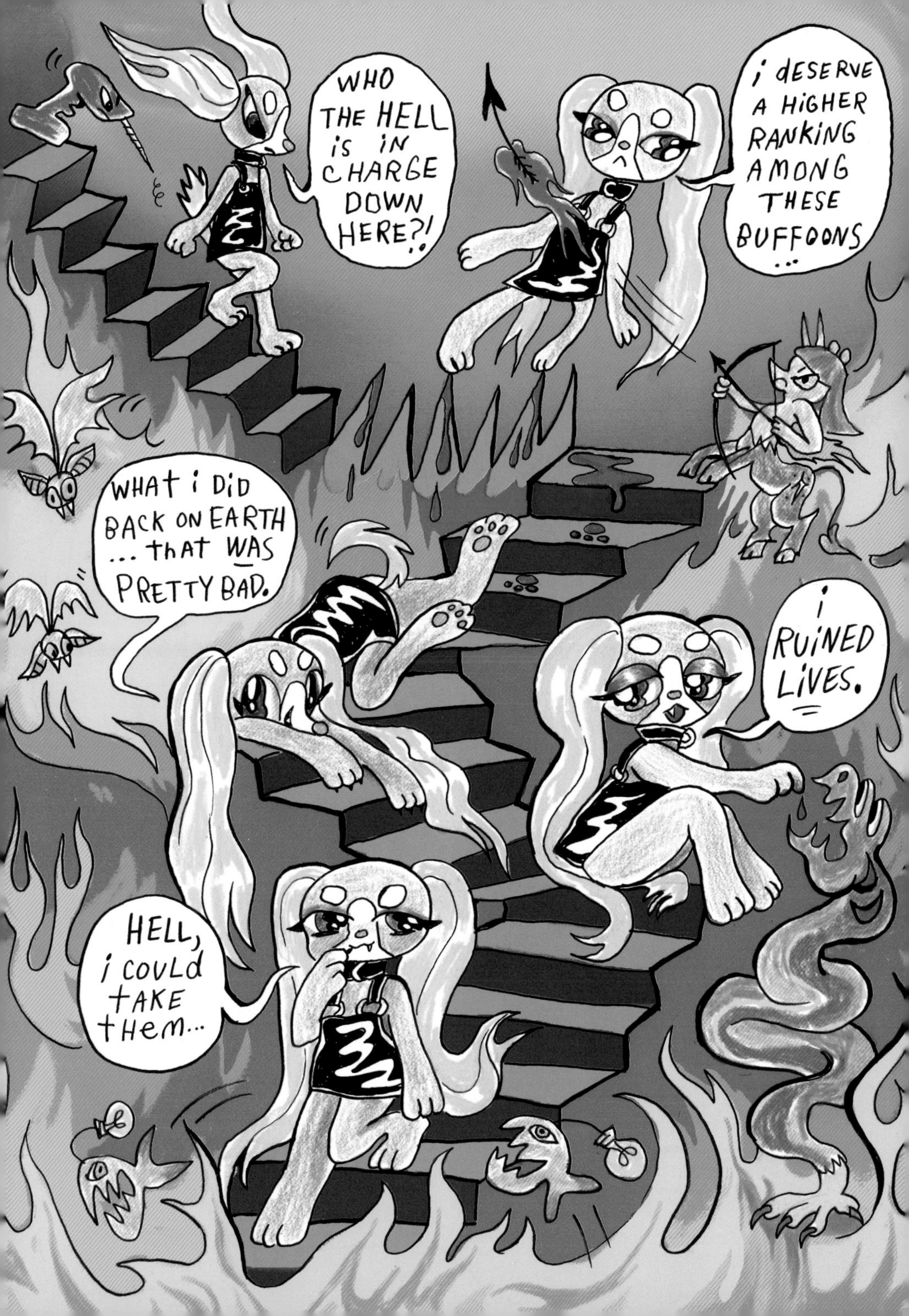
WHO THE HELL is IN CHARGE DOWN HERE?!
i DESERVE A HIGHER RANKING AMONG THESE BUFFOONS ...
WHAT i DID BACK ON EARTH ... THAT WAS PRETTY BAD.
i RUINED LIVES.
HELL, i COULD TAKE THEM...

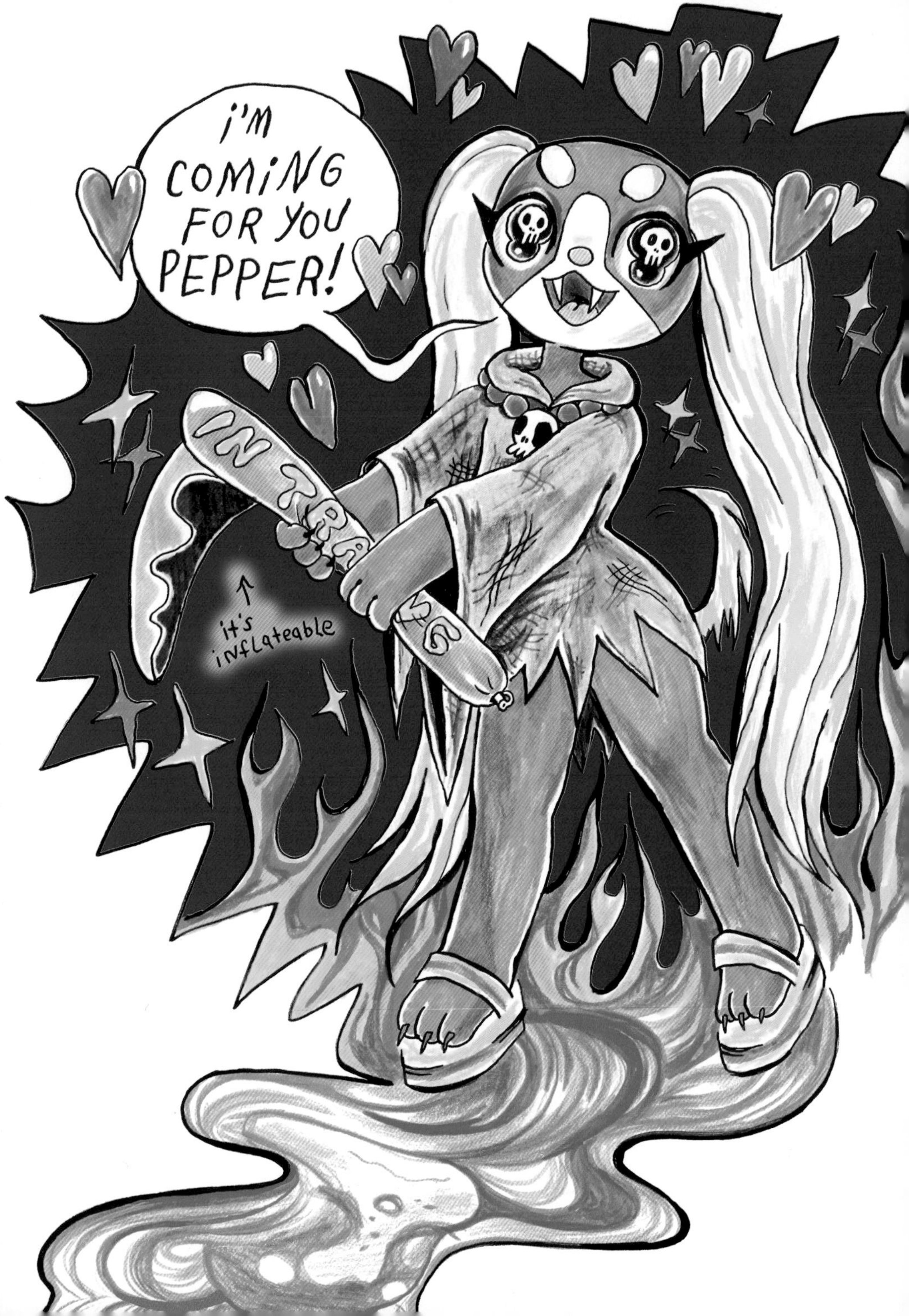
i'M COMING FOR YOU PEPPER!
it's inflateable

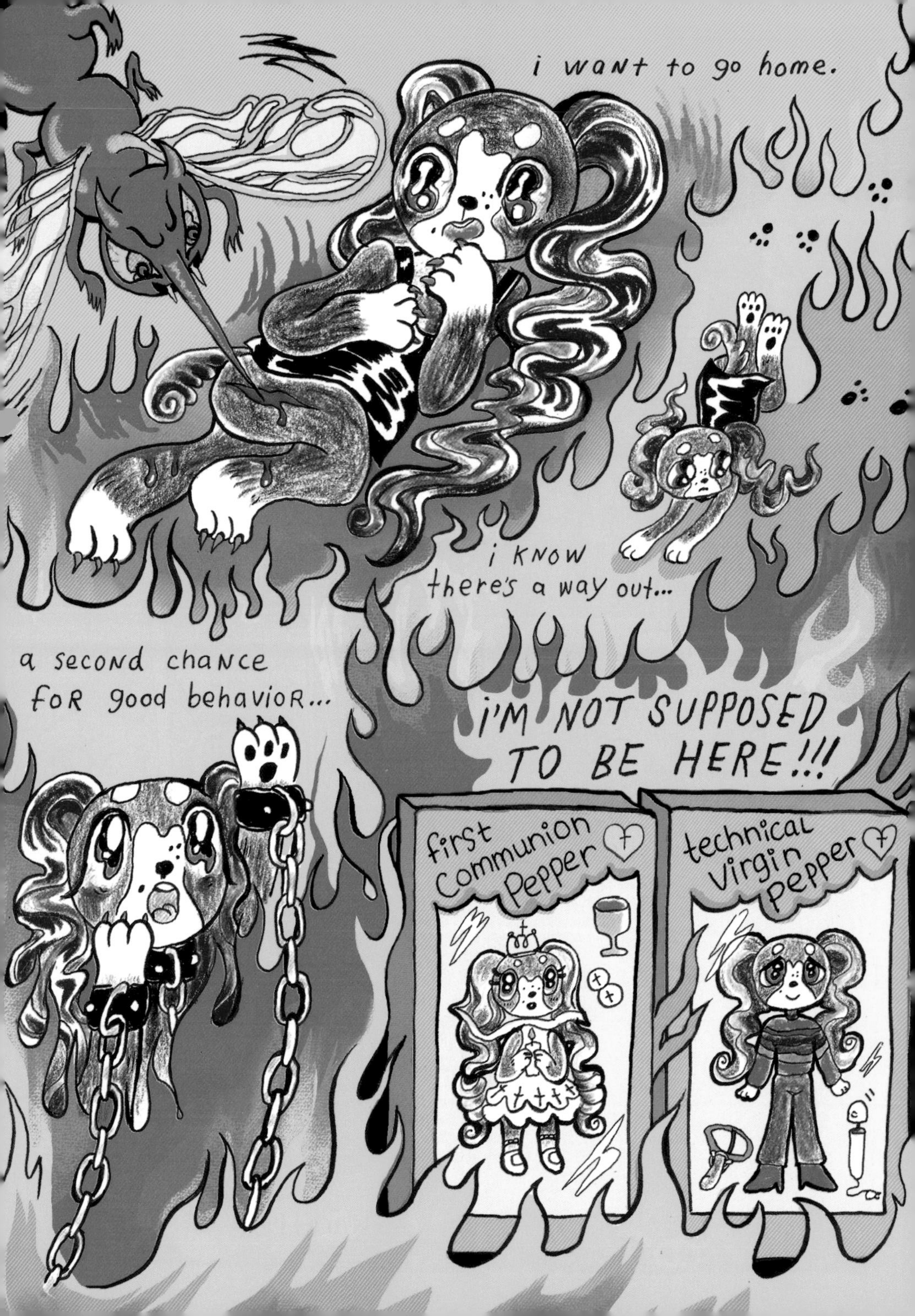

i want to go home.
i know there's a way out...
a second chance for good behavior...
I'M NOT SUPPOSED TO BE HERE!!!
first communion Pepper
technical virgin pepper

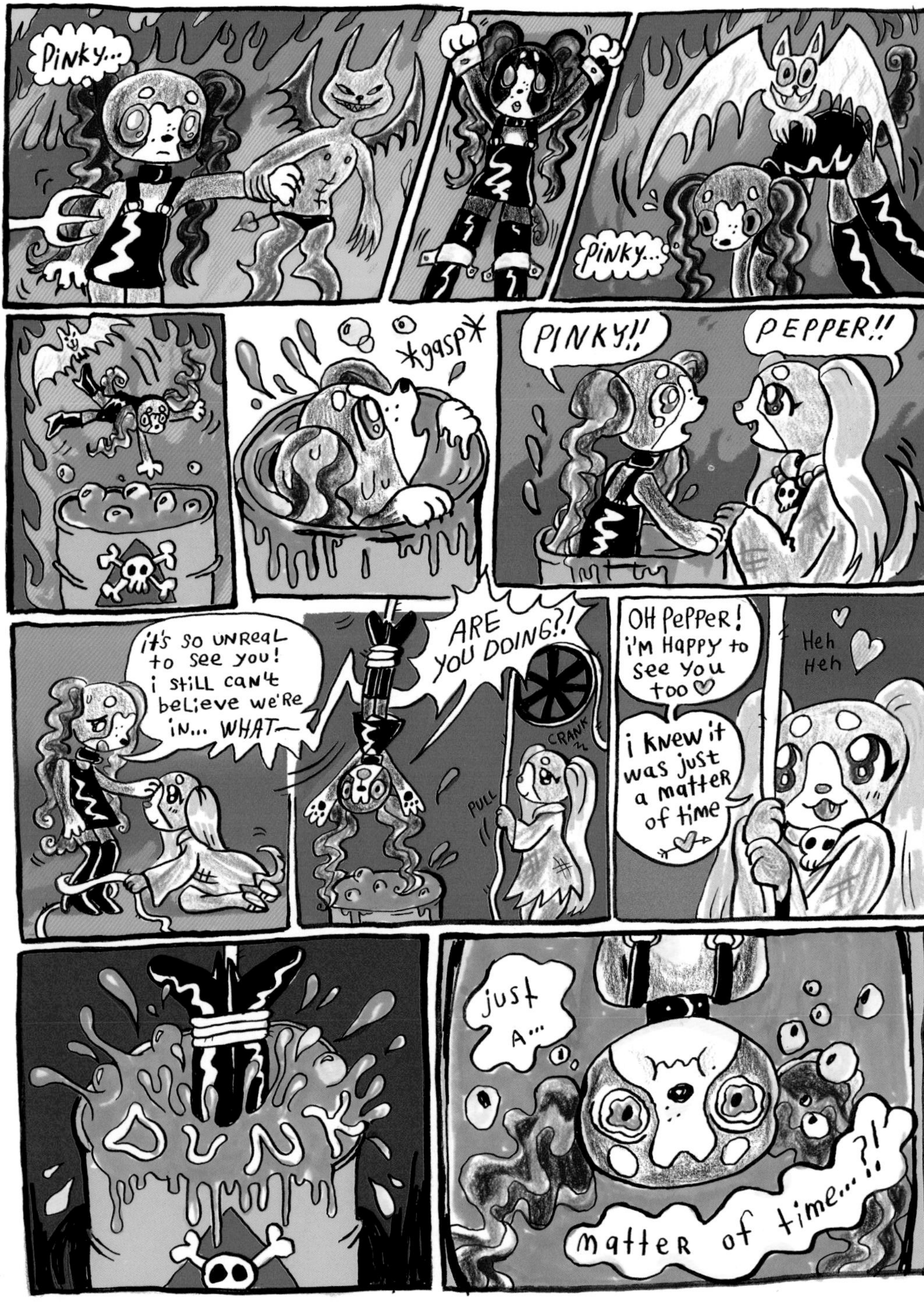

Pinky...
Pinky...
*gasp*
PINKY!!
PEPPER!!
it's so unreal to see you! i still can't believe we're in... WHAT—
ARE YOU DOING?!
CRANK
PULL
OH Pepper! i'm Happy to see You too
Heh Heh
i knew it was just a matter of time
DUNK
just a...
matter of time...?!

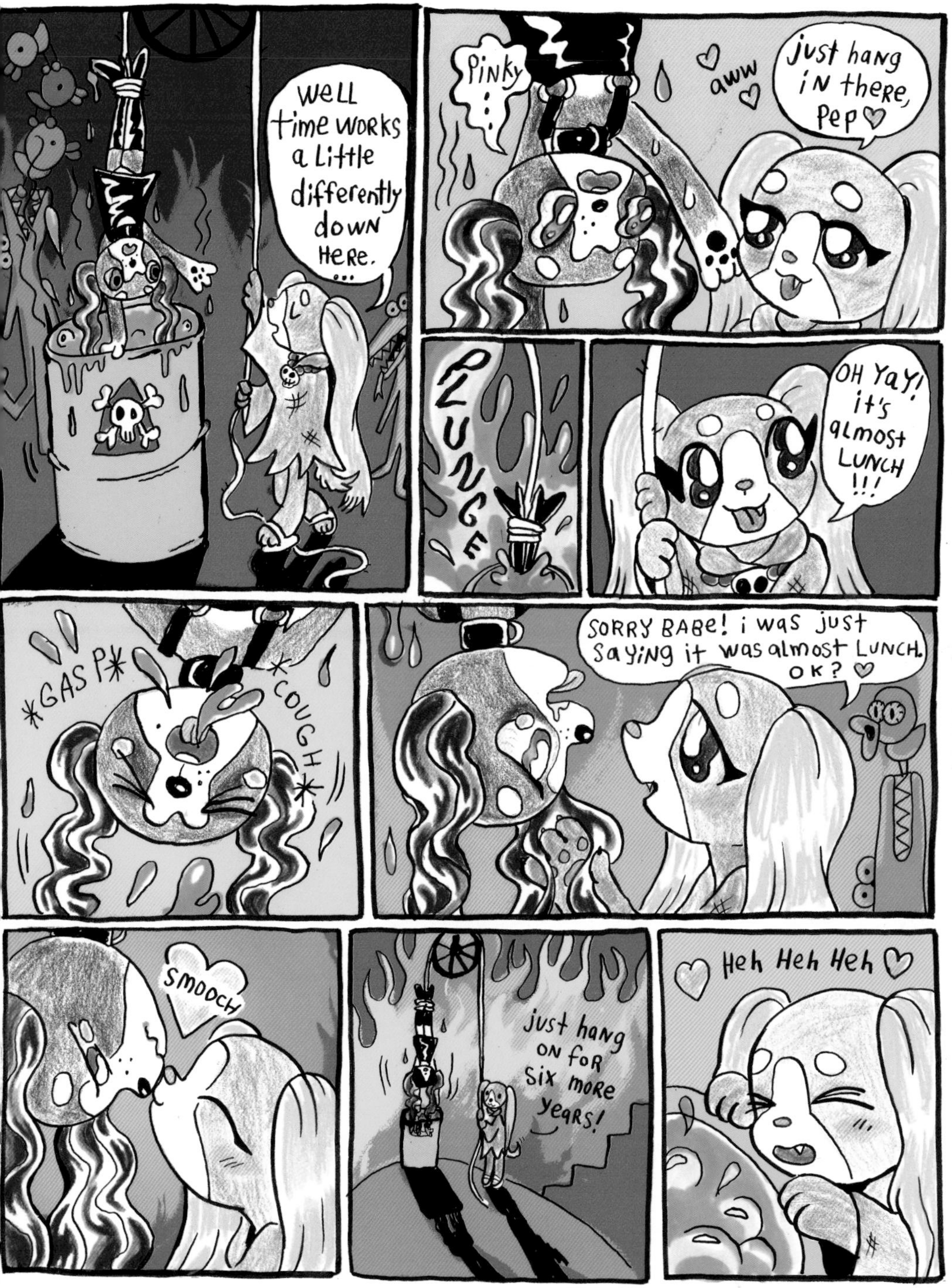
well time works a little differently down here. ...
Pinky ...
aww
just hang in there, Pep
PLUNGE
OH YAY! it's almost LUNCH !!!
*GASP*
*COUGH*
SORRY BABE! i was just saying it was almost LUNCH. OK?
SMOOCH
just hang on for six more years!
Heh Heh Heh

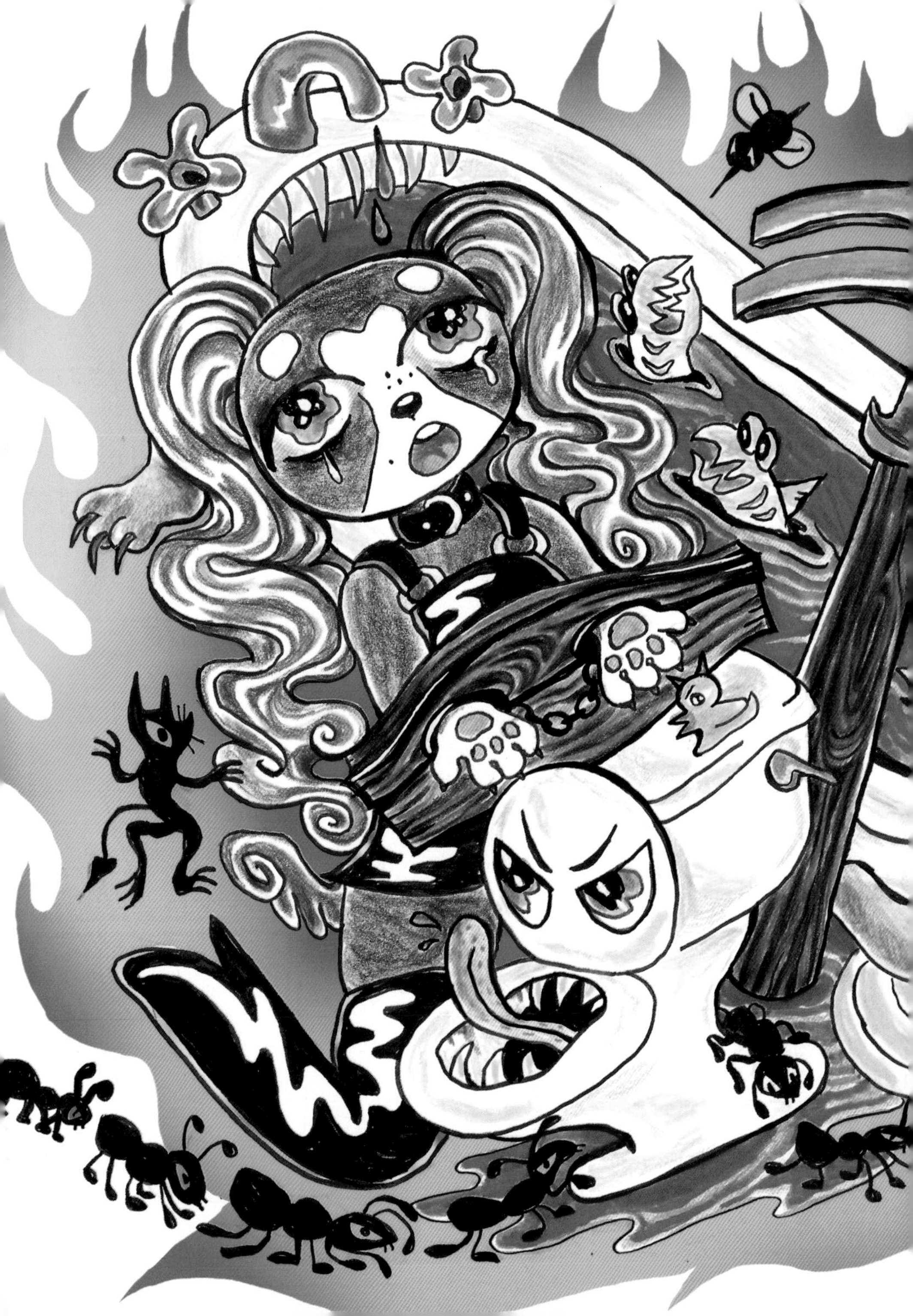

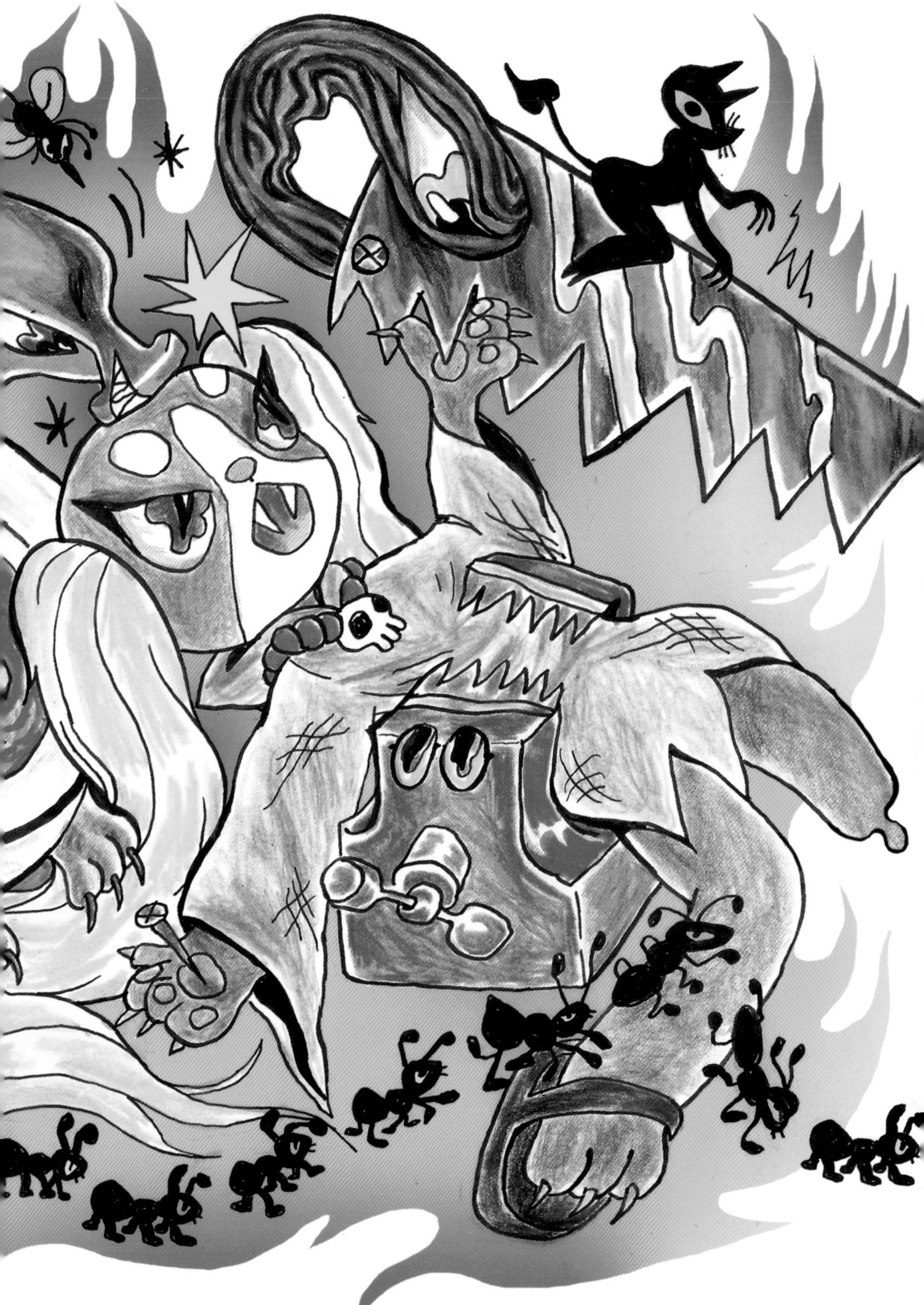

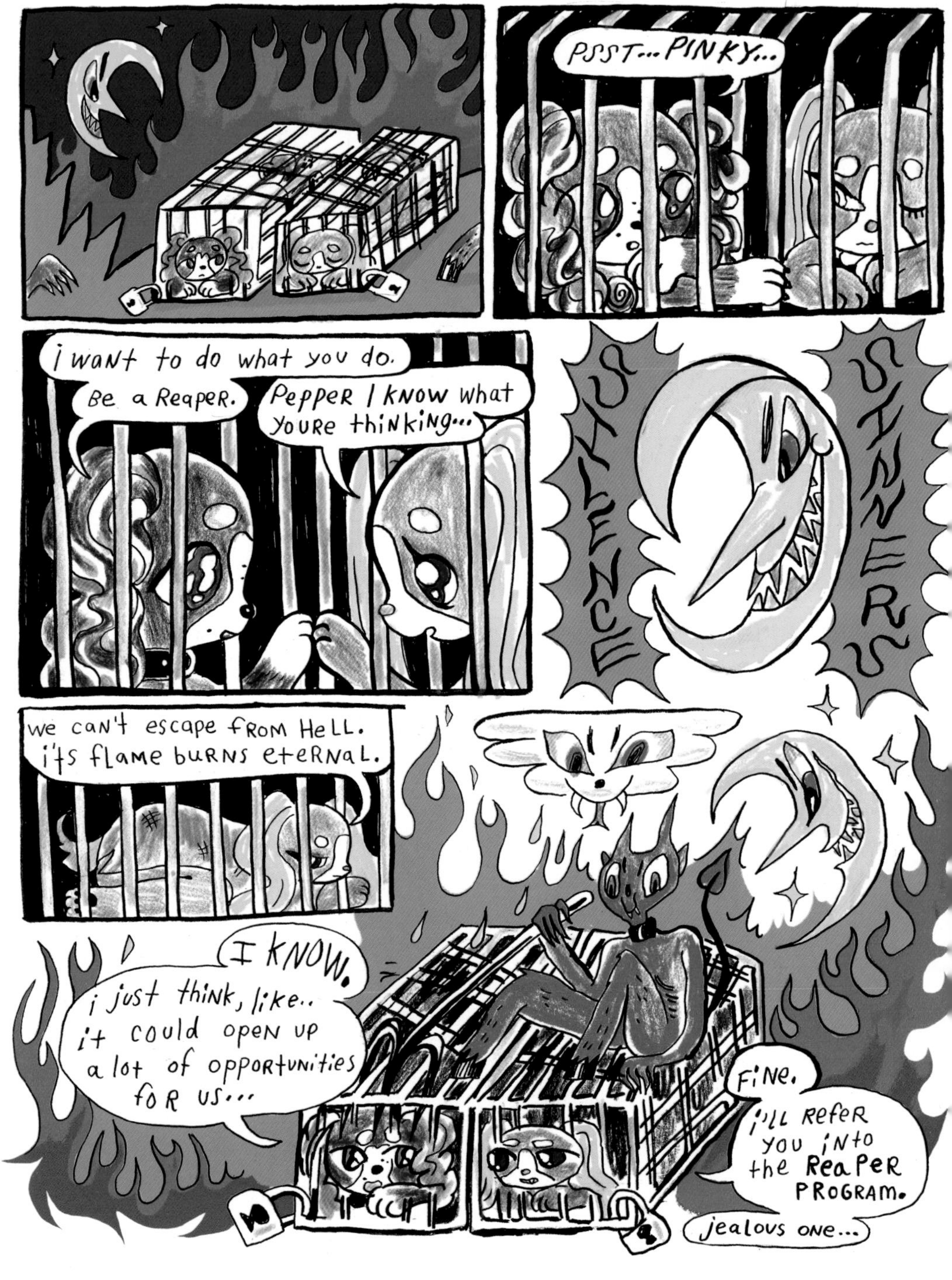
PSST... PINKY...
i want to do what you do.
Be a Reaper.
Pepper I know what youre thinking...
SILENCE
SINNERS
we can't escape from Hell. it's flame burns eternal.
I KNOW.
i just think, like.. it could open up a lot of opportunities for us...
Fine.
i'll refer you into the Reaper PROGRAM.
jealous one...

Pepper's Training

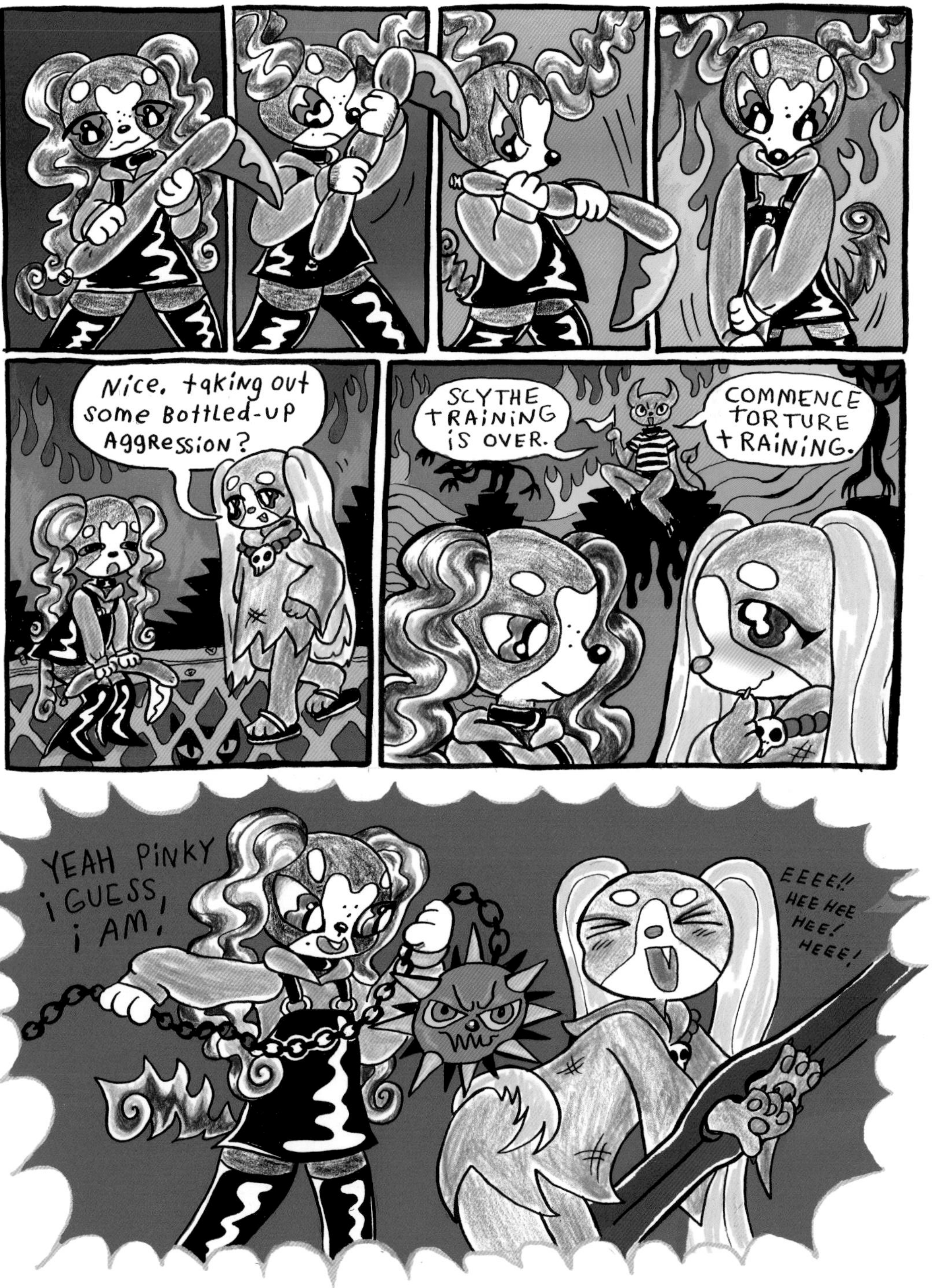
Nice, taking out some Bottled-up Aggression?
SCYTHE TRAINING IS OVER.
COMMENCE TORTURE TRAINING.
YEAH PINKY I GUESS, I AM!
EEEE!! HEE HEE HEE! HEEE!

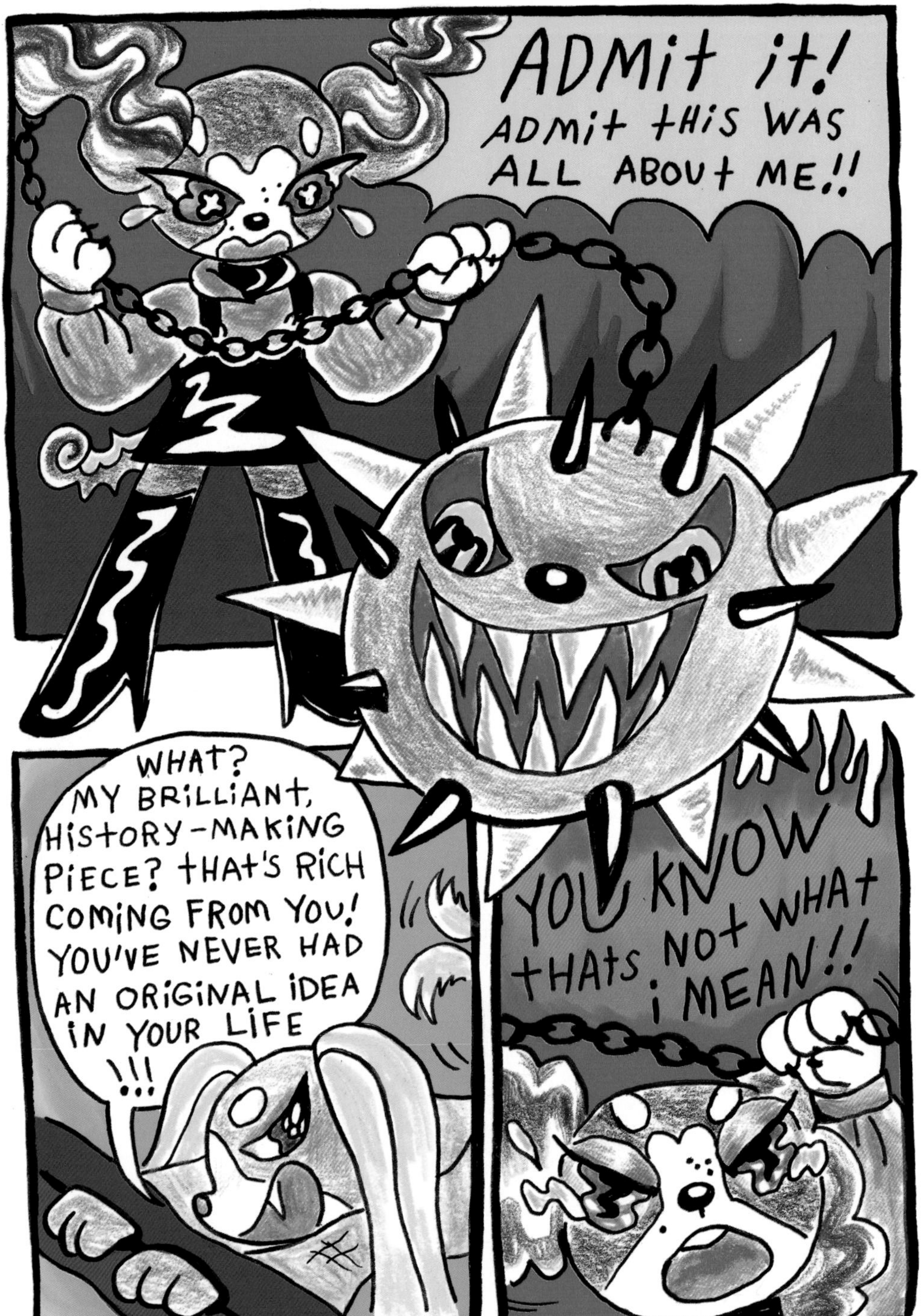
ADMIT it! ADMIT THIS WAS ALL ABOUT ME!!
WHAT? MY BRILLIANT, HISTORY-MAKING PIECE? THAT'S RICH COMING FROM YOU! YOU'VE NEVER HAD AN ORIGINAL IDEA IN YOUR LIFE !!!
YOU KNOW THATS NOT WHAT I MEAN!!

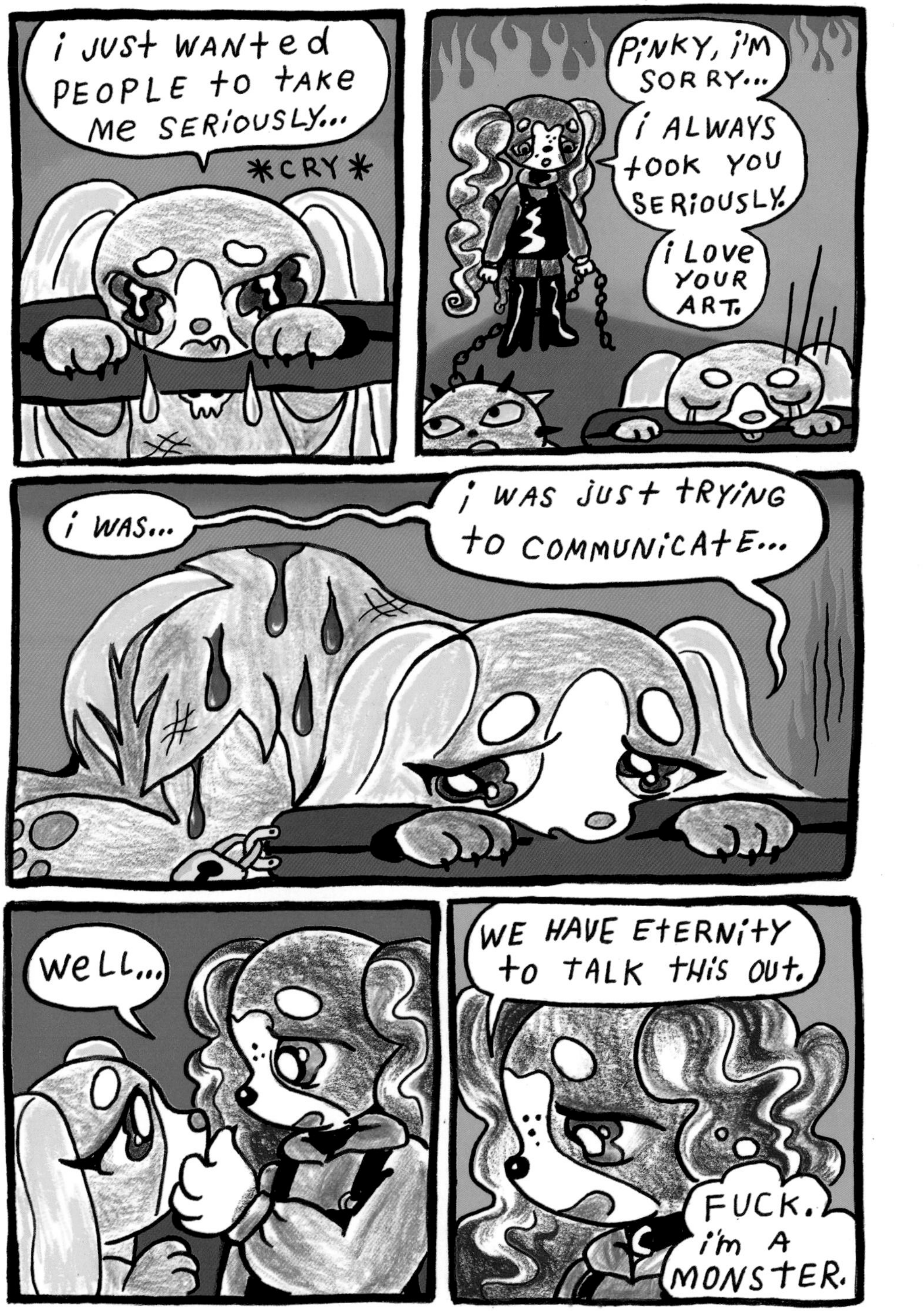
i JUST WANTed PEOPLE to take me SERiOUSLY...
*CRY*
PiNKY, i'M SORRY...
i ALWAYS took YOU SERiOUSLY.
i LOVE YOUR ART.
i WAS...
i WAS JUST tRYiNG to COMMUNiCAtE...
WeLL...
WE HAVE EtERNity to TALK tHiS OUt.
FUCK. i'm A MONSTER.

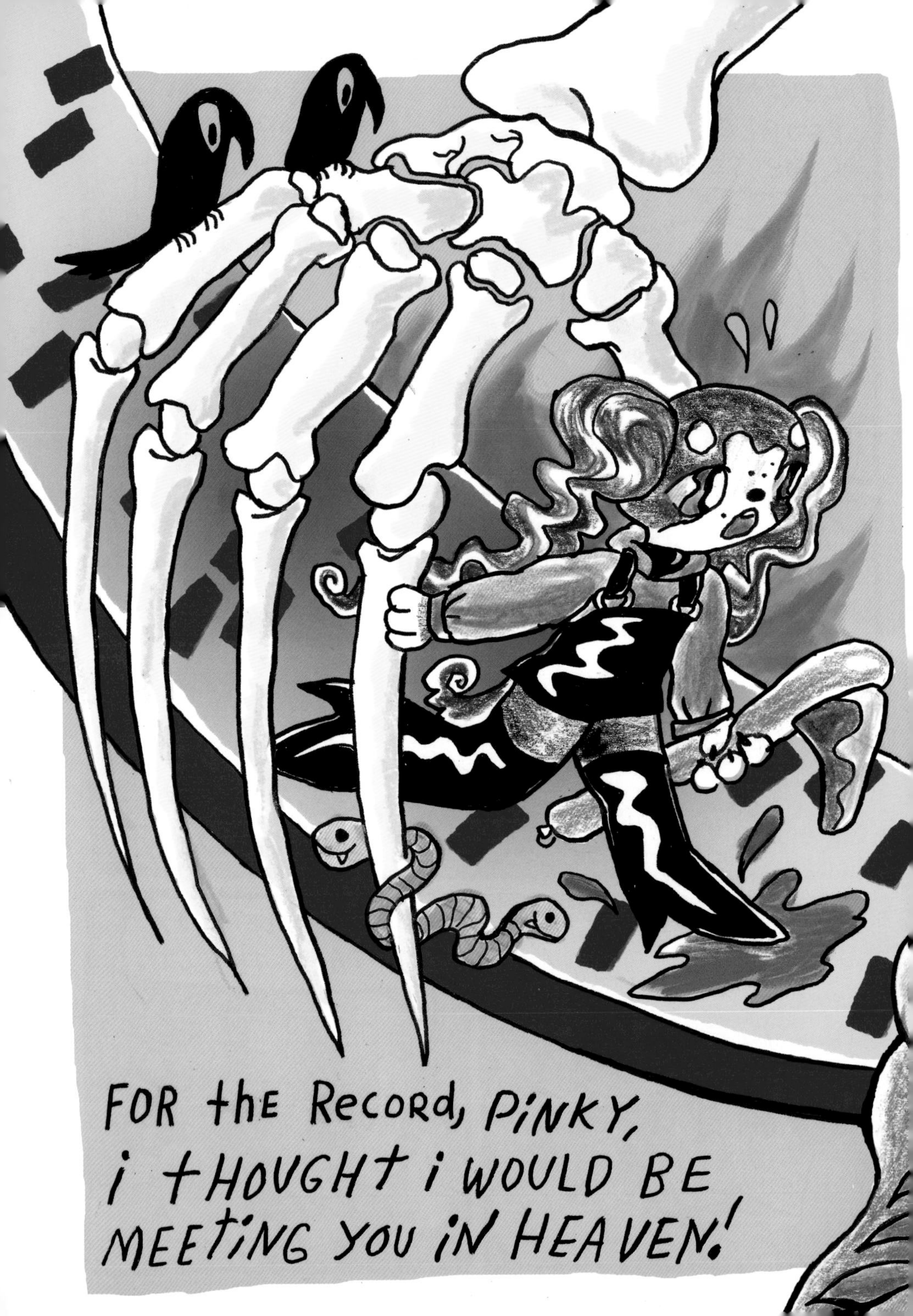
FOR the Record, PINKY,
i THOUGHT i WOULD BE
MEETING YOU iN HEAVEN!

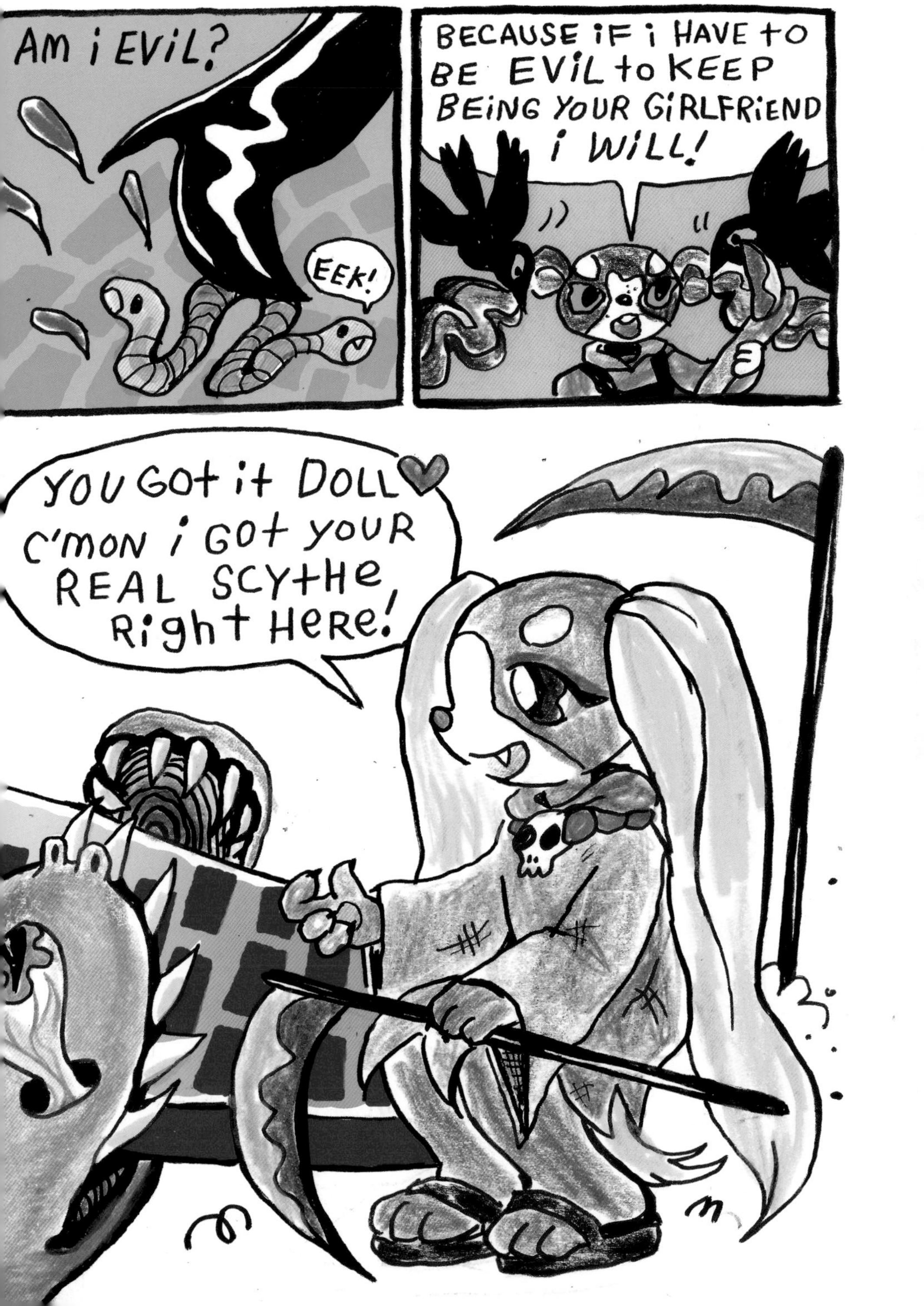
Am i EViL?
EEK!
BECAUSE iF i HAVE to BE EViL to KEEP BEiNG YOUR GiRLFRiEND i WiLL!
YOU GOt it DOLL
C'MON i GOt YOUR REAL SCYtHE, Right HERE!

666 YEARS LATER

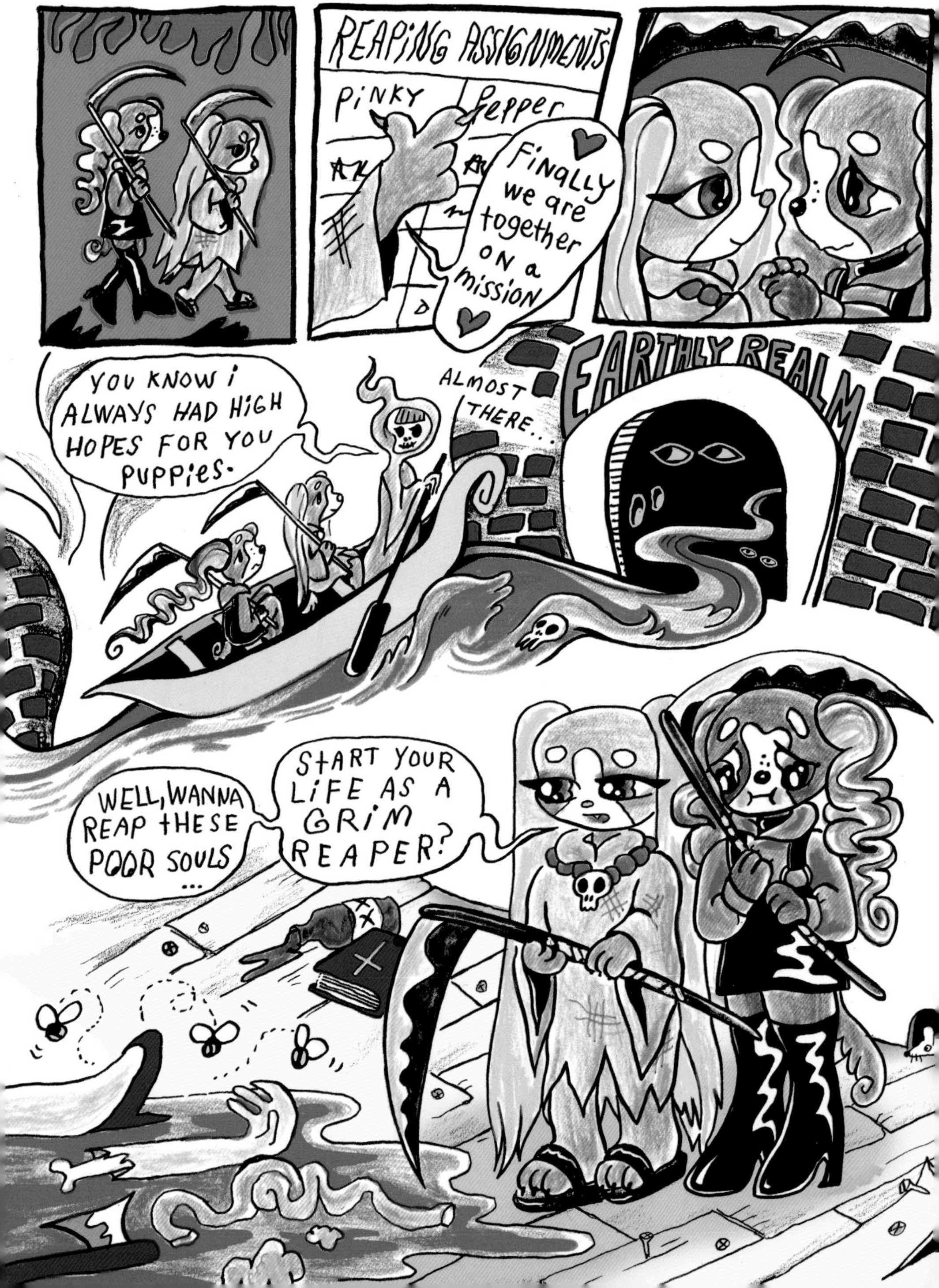
REAPING ASSIGNMENTS
PINKY
Pepper
Finally we are together on a mission
YOU KNOW I ALWAYS HAD HIGH HOPES FOR YOU PUPPIES.
ALMOST THERE...
EARTHLY REALM
WELL, WANNA REAP THESE POOR SOULS ...
START YOUR LIFE AS A GRIM REAPER?

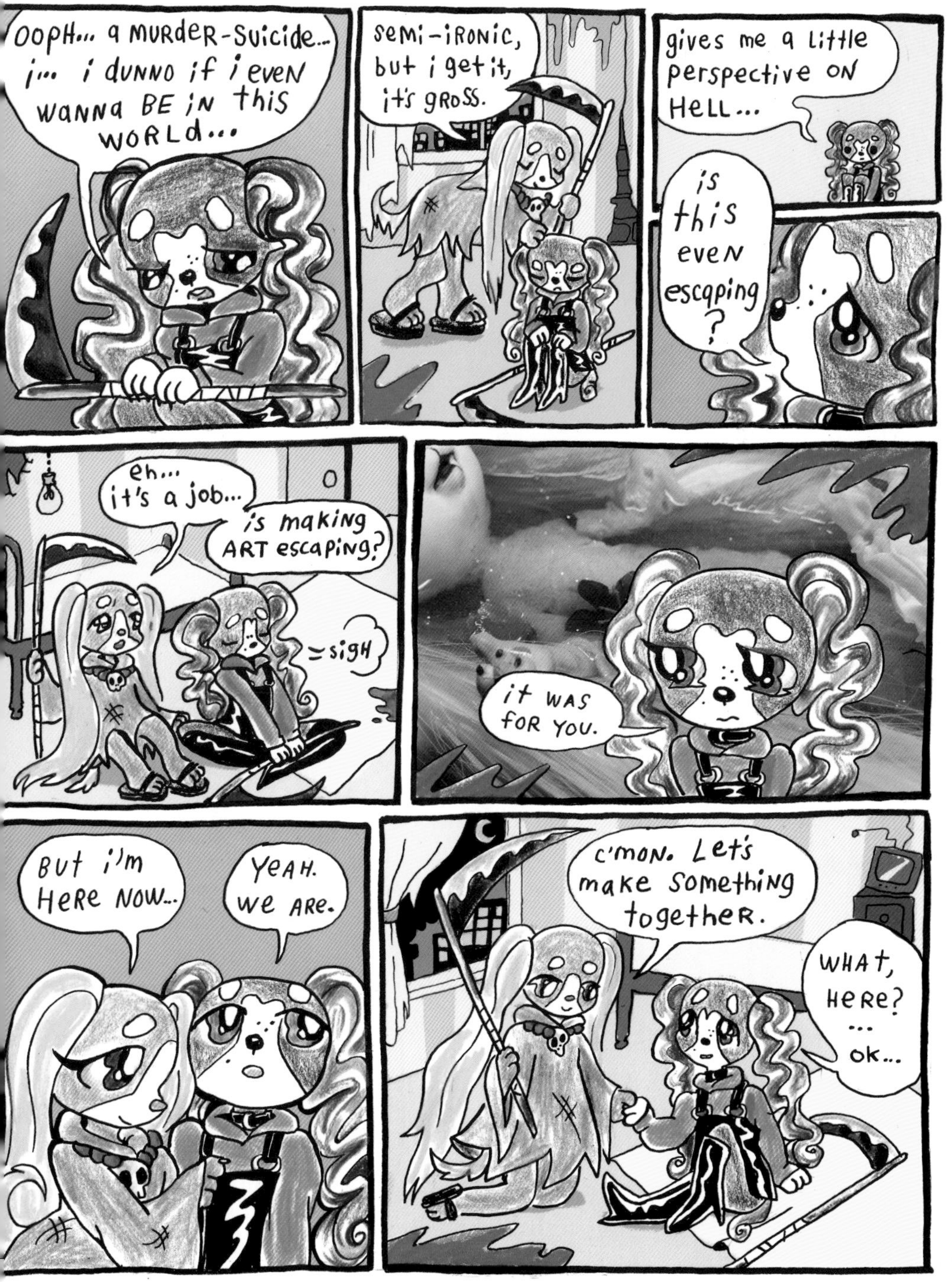

OOPH... a MURDER-SUICIDE... i... i dunno if i even wanna BE in this WORLD...
semi-IRONIC, but i get it, it's GROSS.
gives me a little perspective ON HELL...
is this even escaping ?
eh... it's a job...
is making ART escaping?
sigh
it WAS FOR YOU.
But i'm Here now...
Yeah. we are.
c'mon. Let's make something together.
WHAT, HERE? ... ok...

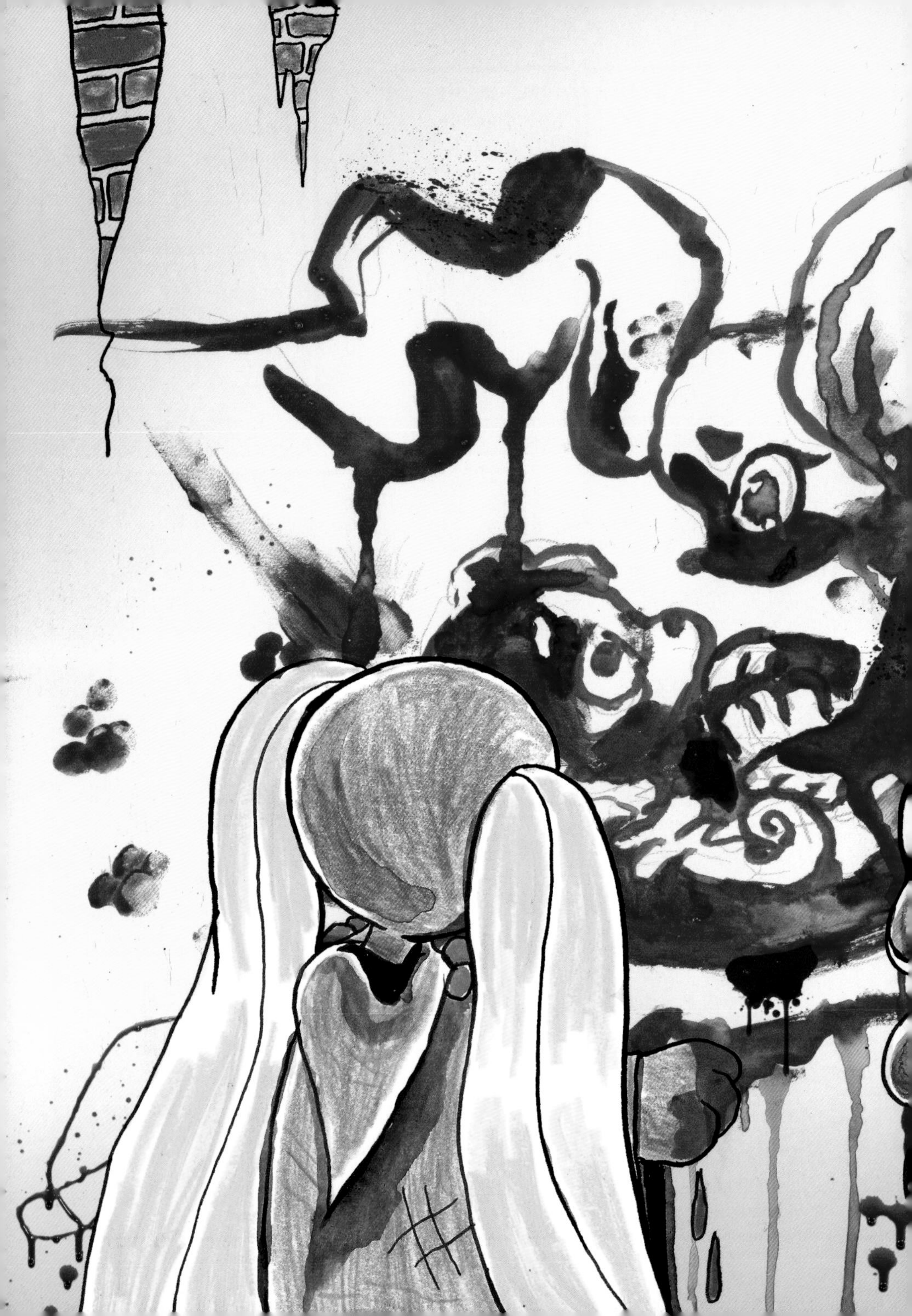

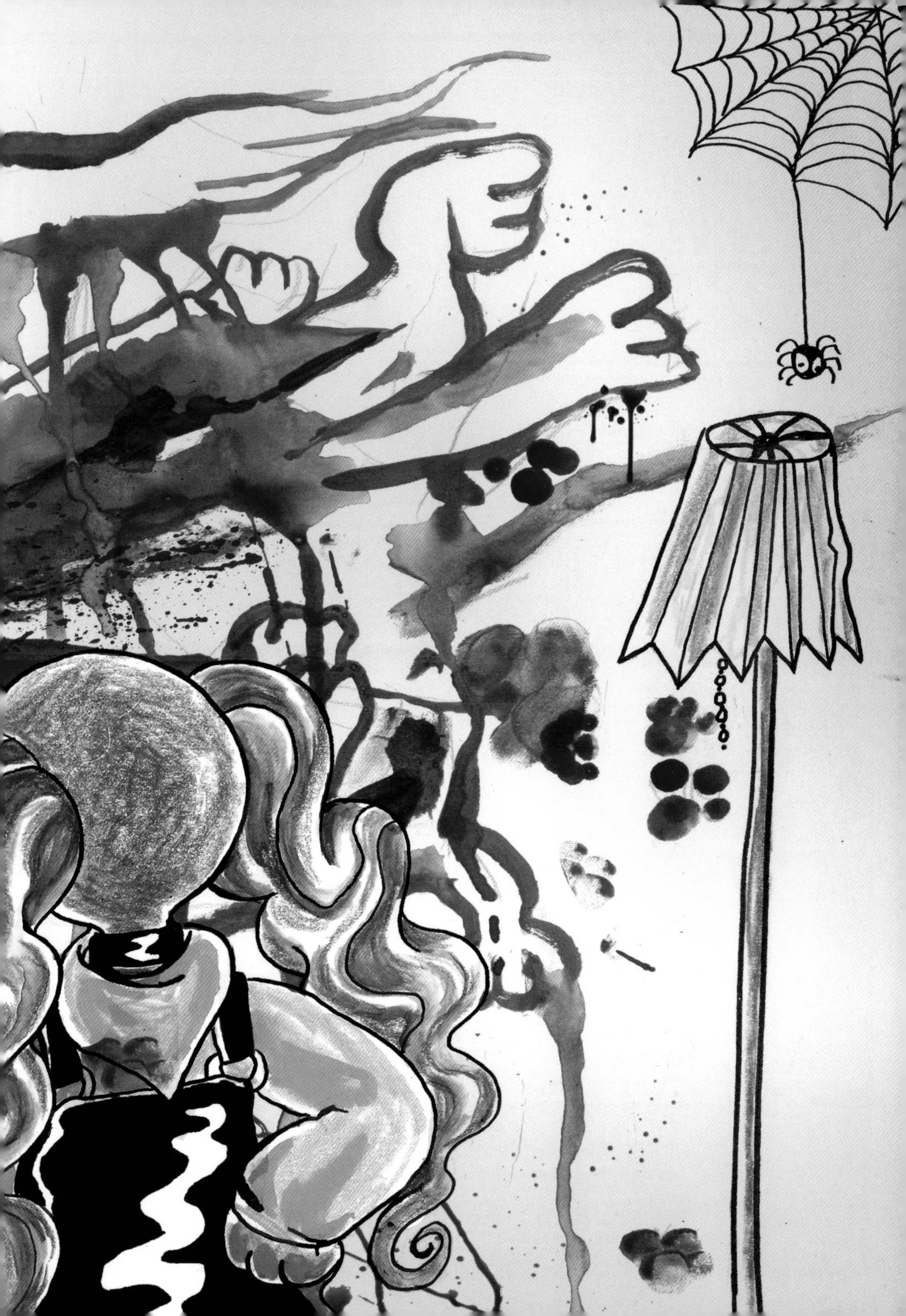

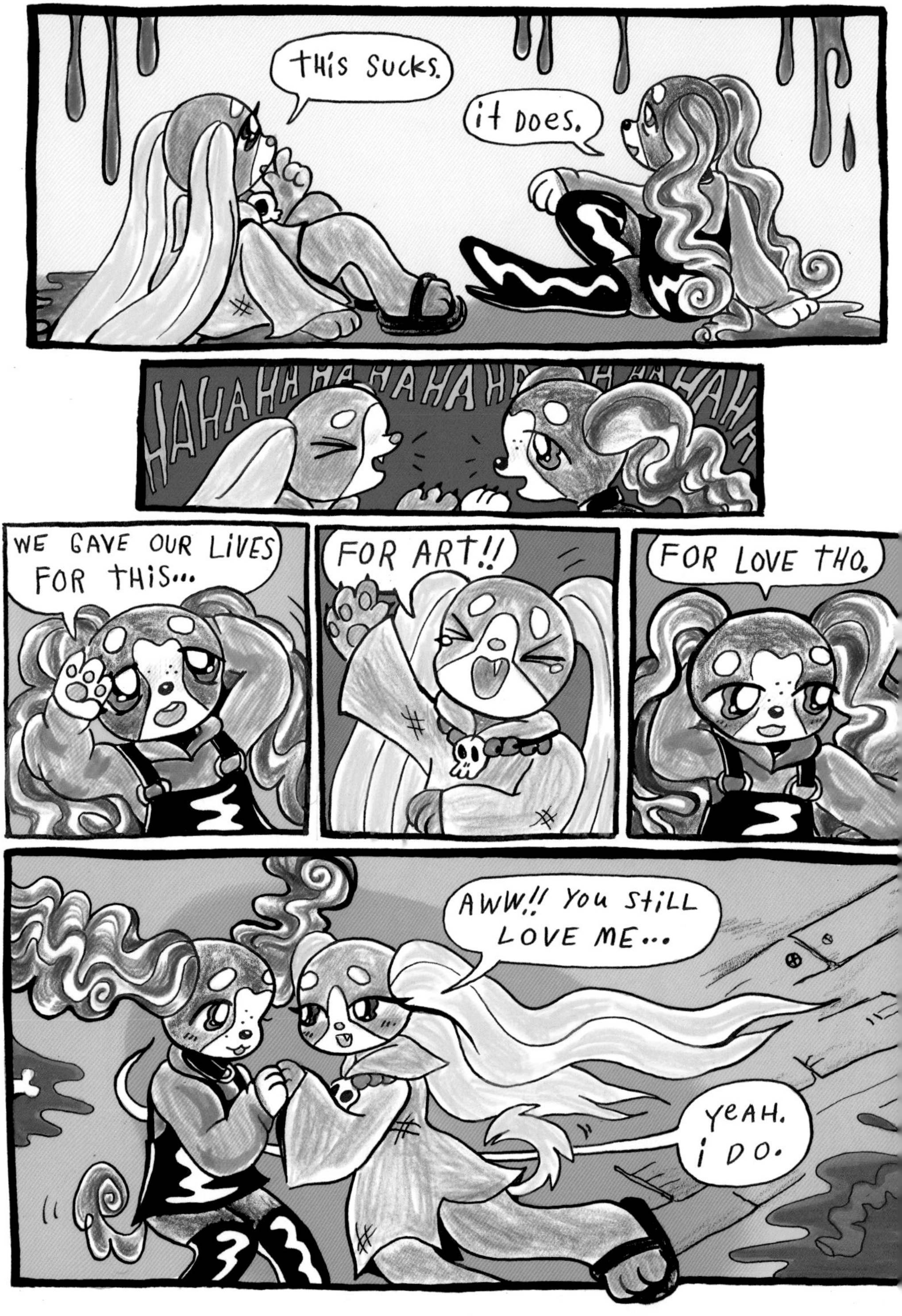
THIS SUCKS.
it DOES.
HAHAHAHAHAHAHAHAHAHAHAHAH
WE GAVE OUR LIVES FOR THIS...
FOR ART!!
FOR LOVE THO.
AWW!! YOU STILL LOVE ME...
YEAH. i DO.

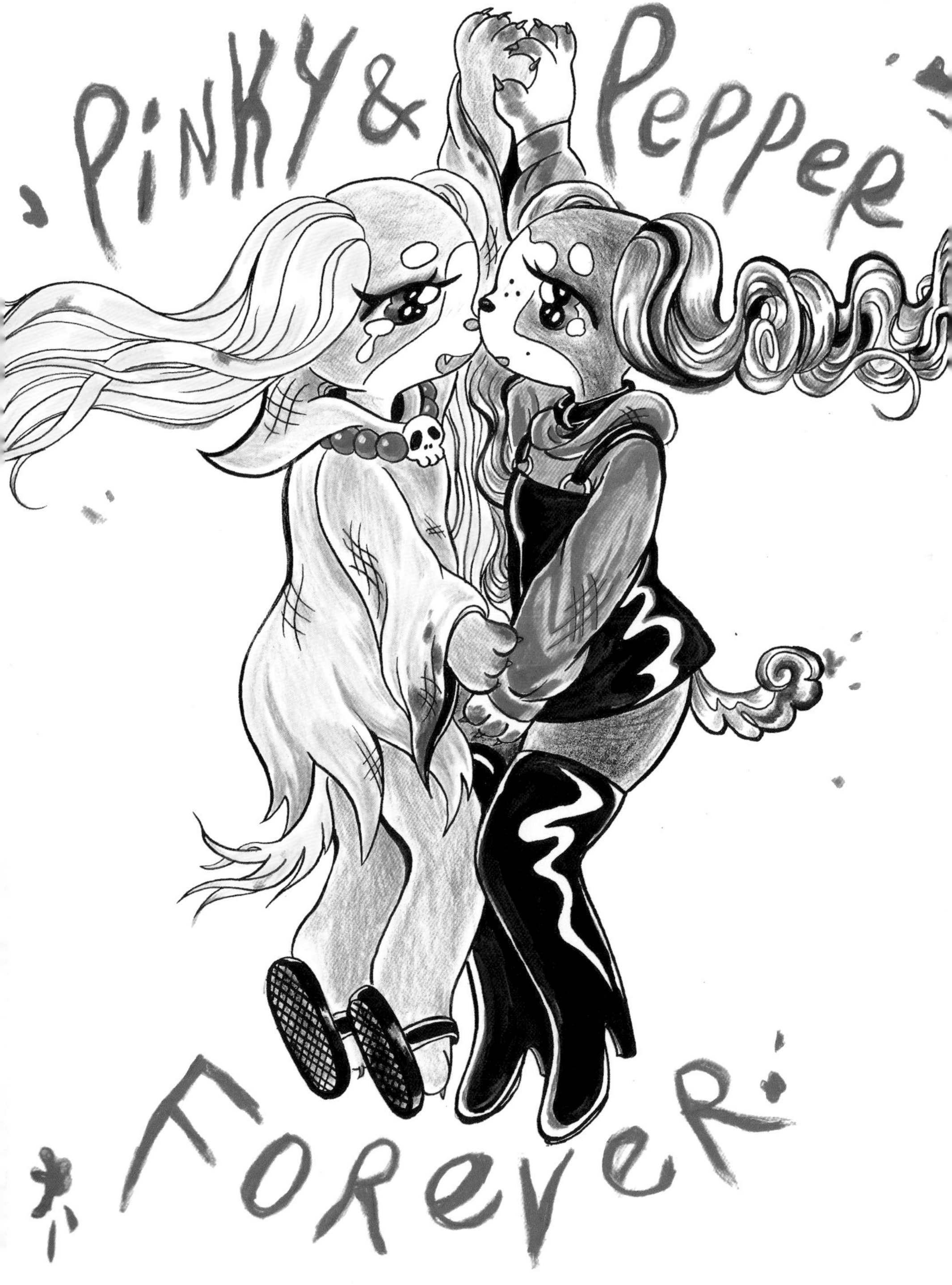
PinKY & PepPeR
FOReveR

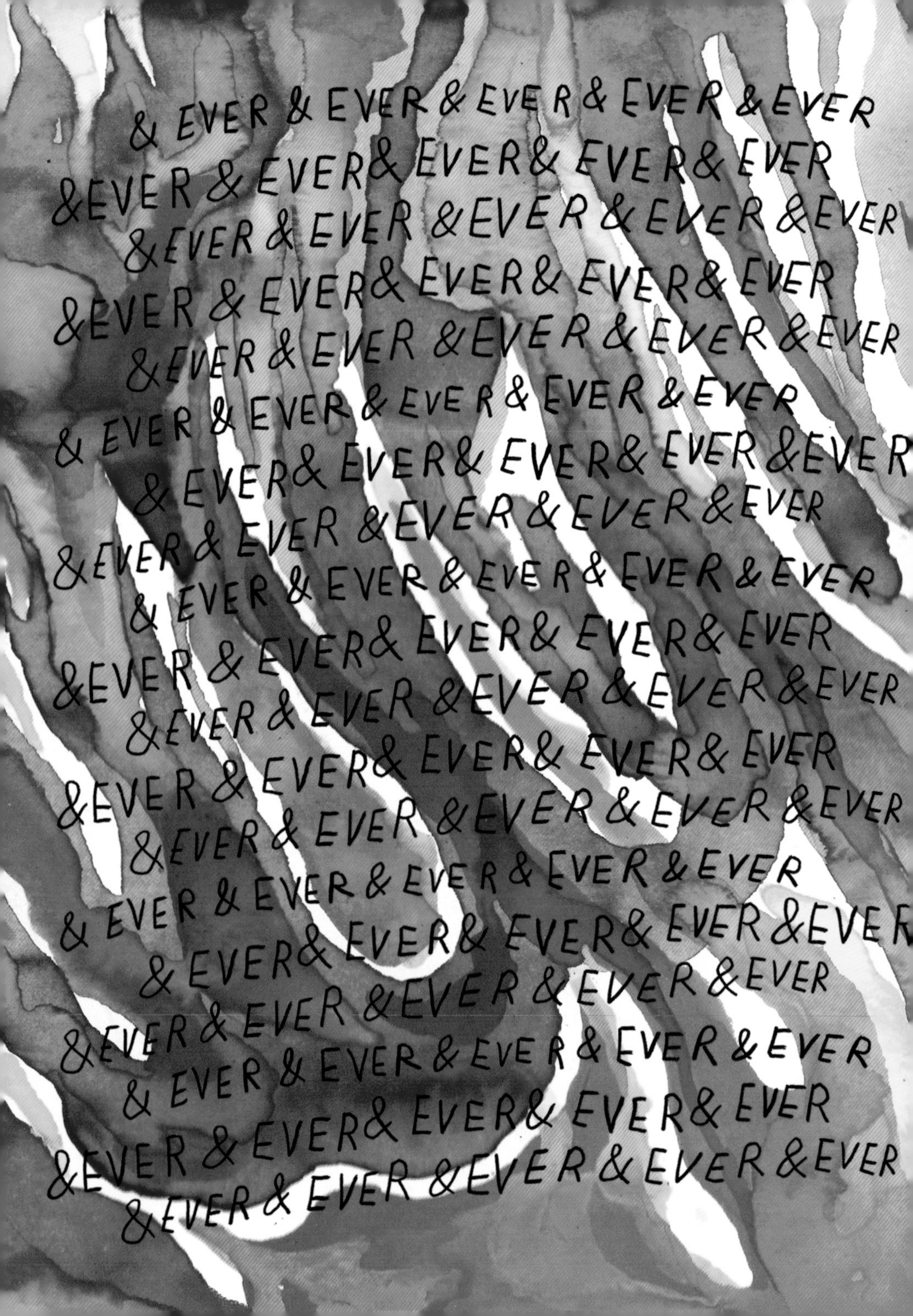
& EVER & EVER & EVER & EVER & EVER
& EVER & EVER & EVER & EVER & EVER
& EVER & EVER & EVER & EVER & EVER
& EVER & EVER & EVER & EVER & EVER
& EVER & EVER & EVER & EVER & EVER
& EVER & EVER & EVER & EVER & EVER
& EVER & EVER & EVER & EVER & EVER
& EVER & EVER & EVER & EVER & EVER
& EVER & EVER & EVER & EVER & EVER
& EVER & EVER & EVER & EVER & EVER
& EVER & EVER & EVER & EVER & EVER
& EVER & EVER & EVER & EVER & EVER
& EVER & EVER & EVER & EVER & EVER
& EVER & EVER & EVER & EVER & EVER
& EVER & EVER & EVER & EVER & EVER
& EVER & EVER & EVER & EVER & EVER
& EVER & EVER & EVER & EVER & EVER
& EVER & EVER & EVER & EVER & EVER
& EVER & EVER & EVER & EVER & EVER
& EVER & EVER

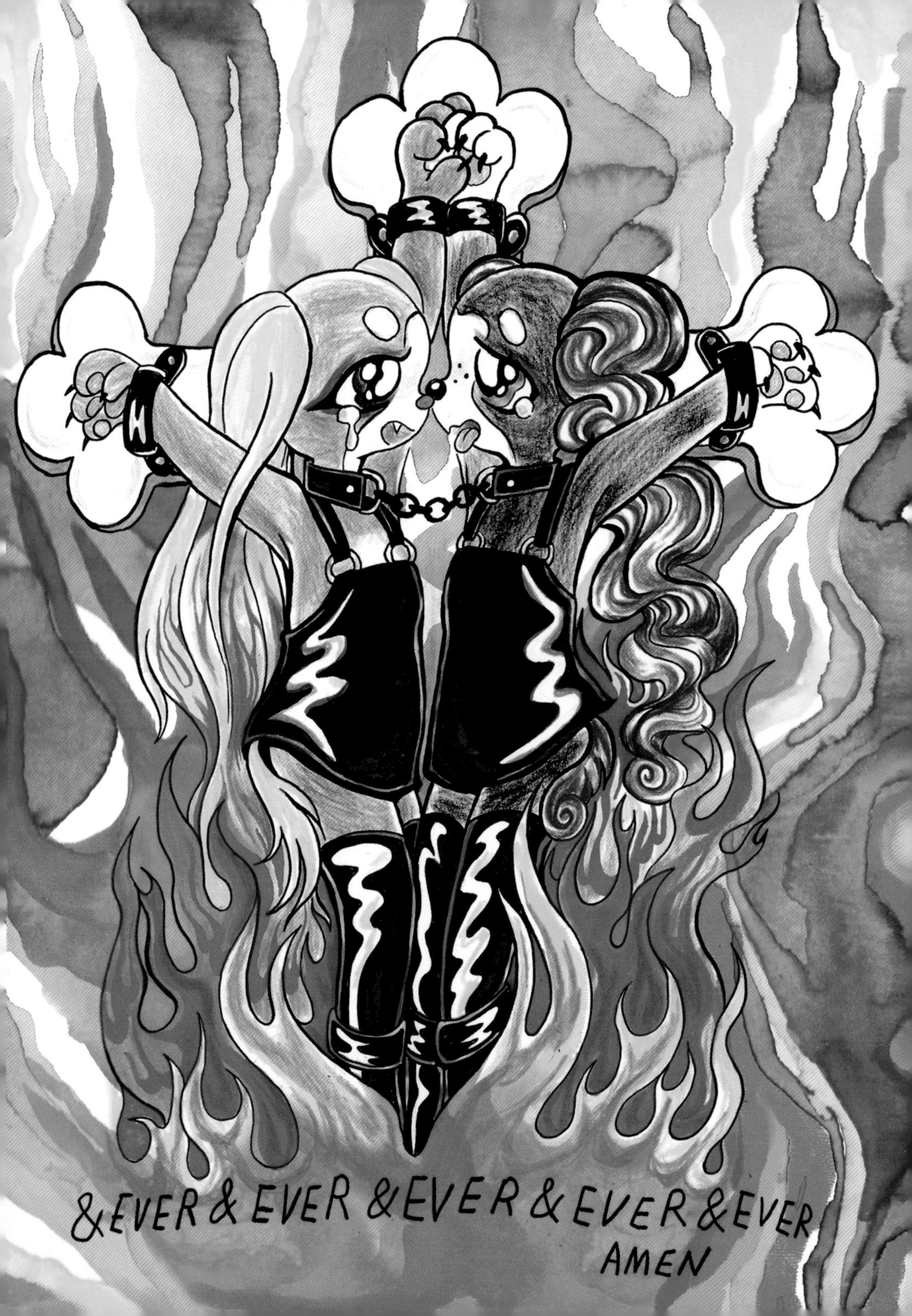
&EVER & EVER &EVER & EVER &EVER
AMEN

# thANK YOU ♡

ARt AssistANts:
e JACKSON, OPAL peNce
& MiNipete

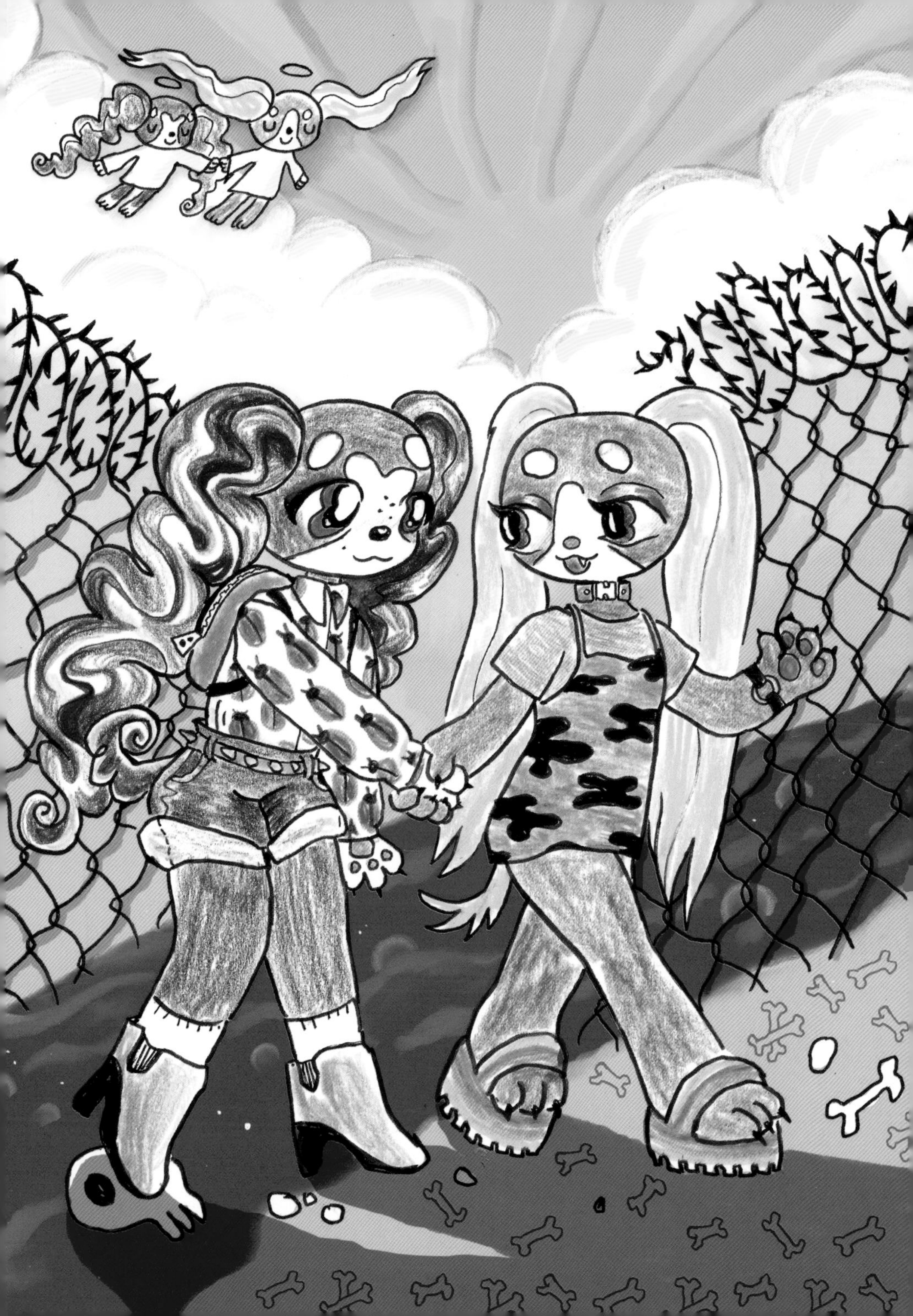